# HORSES
## *in* COMPANY

# HORSES
## *in* COMPANY

### *Lucy Rees*

J.A. ALLEN

First published in 2017 by
JA Allen

JA Allen is an imprint of
The Crowood Press Ltd
Ramsbury, Marlborough
Wiltshire SN8 2HR

**www.crowood.com**

**British Library Cataloguing-in-Publication Data**
A catalogue record for this book is available from the British Library.

ISBN 978 1 90880 956 8

Typeset by Jean Cussons Typesetting, Diss, Norfolk

Printed and bound in India by Replika Press Pvt Ltd

# Contents

# Introduction

This book presents a radically new view of horses' social relations and organization, a view that inevitably affects how we interpret our interactions with horses. It proposes that horses' social life and relations developed in response to the natural selection pressures in their evolution: predators. Horses are prey animals.

In itself, of course, the idea that horses are prey animals is by no means new; we have been paying lip service to it for years. Yet we do not seem to have taken its implications seriously: that it is the focal point of the way horses live together. The current interpretation of their social life is that horses interact according to dominance hierarchies, which have nothing to do with predators.

Throughout many years of working with horses, and especially in resolving problems that arise between horses and people, I had realized that dominance is not a useful concept. Analysing horse-human relations in terms of dominance creates far more problems than it solves. The same has been found to be true of dog-human relations.

However, until a few years ago I had no alternative theory or way of analysing social interactions, although having dispensed with dominance as a factor, others started to become clear and useful in practice: the horse's acute awareness of our body language, his cooperation, his dislike of physical restriction and, above all, his coordination with others, whether horse or human. But they did not come together as a coherent picture. I lacked a paradigm.

I arrived at the new paradigm through observations of feral horses and especially of their behaviour in the face of predator attack, a curiously neglected field of equine ethology. Gradually I came to see that their whole social organization and relations reflect their adaptation to the ever-present possibility of predator attack. The exact ways in which they behave to escape successfully are reflected in their everyday lives – even those of domestic horses that have no practical experience of predators.

This is an ethological approach: why do animals behave the way they do?

I would like this book to be accessible to those many thoughtful and intelligent horsepeople who have no base in ethology (as well as those who do). I have therefore thought it necessary to start with a brief explanation of some of the ideas that are used later in the book. This is not a potted ethology textbook but a way to avoid breaking a logical flow with explanations of the concepts used.

Behaviour helps an animal stay alive and pass on its genes to the next generation in its own natural environment, in various ways. Some behaviour has a strong genetic basis, and is acted upon by natural selection just as the exact form of an animal's body is.

Therefore, we must look at the selection pressures revealed in the course of horse evolution. Predators, of course, are one.

The classic and important studies of feral horse behaviour show that they all adopt more or less the same solution to life's problems, and introduce us to some terms and concepts. These studies help us see what behaviour is constant in all natural contexts. Although I have not wanted to delve deeply into domestic horse behaviour and lose the thread of the story, I hope that thoughtful horse-owners will find much to reflect on.

My own studies, which come next, have not been published before. Since the exact conditions and methods of study can influence results, scientists are careful to detail them, which often makes boring reading to the non-specialist. I've tried to convey a more living picture of what it is like to be a field ethologist; the interactions in the herd, the extreme efforts that horses make to avoid competitive conflict, the questions that arise and the ethological approach to answers.

Thus prepared with a general picture, we can examine exactly what happens, and why, when attack comes. My understanding of my observations owes much to an up-and-coming field of research that has not been applied to horses before but is providing great insights into herd, flock and shoal behaviour, using behavioural algorithms for self-organizing group movement.

What then became clear to me is that the factors that govern successful escape also govern social interactions and organization within a band or herd in more peaceful moments, too. We see that social behaviour is adaptive, following a coherent logic given that horses are prey animals. Within feral bands they do not compete against each other but collectively against predators, and maintain social relations that allow them to behave appropriately and instantly in the face of situations, grading from changing their maintenance activity to life-threatening attack.

This hypothesis, or paradigm, since it changes the way we interpret social relations and organization, is based on my own observations, which, for practical reasons, tend to be more qualitative than quantitative. They do, however, suggest a large number of testable questions that, I fervently hope, will be examined more fully in future research.

The paradigm I propose is not the generally promoted and accepted one: that horses interact according to dominance hierarchies. There are serious flaws, including a lack of consistent evidence, in the ethological arguments for dominance hierarchies; there is also a wide gulf between what ethologists mean by dominance and what the general public means by it. A critical examination of these problems therefore follows.

Yet the concept of dominance is so deep-rooted in equestrianism, and indeed seems so self-evident to many horse-owners, that we also need to consider whether there are alternative explanations for the behaviour that we see. We find that there are many reasons why we interpret things in certain ways, even when these are not true. In the same way, we see the sun rise in the east and set in the west; even when we know we are perched on a rolling ball, we find that fact difficult to appreciate.

Finally, we consider some of the implications of this change of paradigm, both ethologically and in our daily interactions with horses.

## CHAPTER 1

# Thinking About Behaviour

Behaviour is adaptive. It helps an animal survive and leave its genetic mark on the world through its offspring. Cats' claws, bats' echolocation, fishes' fins and horses' tails, or any other of the myriad physical adaptations that enable an animal to survive in its particular way of life, would be of no advantage if the animal did not use them properly.

A great deal of behaviour is hard-wired, under genetic control. Natural selection operates on this innate behaviour as it does on the genes that govern bodily form, weeding out the animals that do not behave appropriately in their natural environment and leaving the ones that do to pass on their genes to their descendants.

The simplest form of hard-wired behaviour is reflex action. You do not have to think about contracting your iris when emerging from a dark room into bright sunlight, or how hard you need to push against the ground (and with which muscles) to stay upright. On a more complex level, you do not need to think before avoiding a blow coming at your face, if you see it in time. The response is automatic.

Many animals, insects for instance, operate on this automatic level, which is not necessarily simple: their behaviour can reach remarkable complexity, as it does in ants and bees. Karl von Frisch, who with Niko Tinbergen and Konrad Lorenz won the Nobel Prize in 1973, unravelled the secrets of the honeybee's communication regarding a source of nectar, a remarkably cleverly coded dance on the surface of a comb in the hive. His classic book *The Dancing Bees* describes the observations and experiments that helped him arrive at his conclusions.

This type of automatic behaviour, involving the whole animal in chunks of behaviour rather than single actions, is what was generally called instinctive behaviour, Lorenz and Tinbergen's particular field of study.

These two, ethology's great founder fathers, set out to make a science of ethology, to find the unifying mechanisms underlying instinctive behaviour. They had a long-lasting friendship and collaboration, the immense fruitfulness of which lay partly in their shared interests and partly in their differences in approach. Tinbergen was primarily a naturalist and bird-watcher: he watched animals in their natural habitats, fascinated by the wealth of adaptations that their behaviour showed to different ways of life. Lorenz shared his life and farm with a variety of domestic and tamed animals that he observed and experimented with, delightfully described in *King Solomon's Ring* (1949). He had, then, more opportunity to see how instinctive behaviour, adapted to cope with situations occurring in an animal's natural life, could misfire when the animal found itself in situations outside that lifestyle: in domesticity, for instance.

Working mostly on birds and fish, the two saw that standardized little chunks of behaviour could be triggered or 'released' by specific stimuli – a colour, a movement, a sound – that all animals of the same species reacted to in the same way, without having to learn how to do so. Both the recognition of the releasing stimulus and the reaction were inborn, innate, built into the wiring in some kind of way.

Lorenz, eager to give ethology a theoretical base, invented a mechanical model of instinct. He saw that, sometimes, the longer the animal had been without performing a particular little chunk of behaviour, the more easily this was released, and incorporated this feature into his model.

Scientists love models. Models can be formulae, drawings, flow diagrams or, as in Lorenz's case, a hypothetical structure. Models can be tested by experiment or observation to see if they really work in all cases. Lorenz's did not. The result was years of investigation and argument about whether all instincts worked the same, about what physical neurological structures could correspond to the various parts of his model, about whether this experiment really tested what it claimed to have done, and the like. Eventually the model and even the term instinct were dropped. 'Innate', the term now used, had no historical connotations or pitfalls about assumptions; it correctly implies that this type of behaviour has a hereditary base common to all animals of one particular species.

No one ever said Lorenz did not see what he said he saw: what they debated was his interpretation of his observations. Ethological observations are 'clean': they state baldly what the animal did, when and where, excluding interpretations of why. 'The horse tried to kill the man' is not an ethological observation. 'The horse repeatedly struck the fallen man with his

*Fig. 1.1   The new-born foal does not have a concept of searching for milk: he has an innate urge to put his head between two pillars capped by a shadow. Often, as here, this urge brings him no benefit. But when by chance he is rewarded by milk, he soon learns which two legs to aim for.*

forefoot' is nearer the mark, but is improved by adding the circumstances: 'the man threw stones violently at a horse trapped in an alley. The man stumbled and fell. The horse repeatedly struck the fallen man with his forefoot.' Such an observation, like so many, is open to various interpretations.

Lorenz was an ethologist. His observations were valid even though his model failed, and later theories or models had to explain them.

Tinbergen was less inclined towards proposing universal theories, and more to finding out exactly what happened. He set about investigating what were the properties of a releasing stimulus that made it innately recognizable, and how exact they had to be. When parent herring gulls arrive at the nest, the chicks peck at their beaks and the parents regurgitate food for them. Tinbergen found that what stimulated the chicks to peck was not the parent or the food, but a red spot on the bill. He painted a stick white, painted a red spot on it and moved it up and down in front of a nestful of chicks. If the spot was the right colour, in the right place and the stick moved at the right rate and angle, they pecked; if not, they did not. Nothing even faintly resembling a parent bird was necessary.

Foals are born with an innate urge to get to their feet. They then look between two upright pillars capped by dark shadow. They are not looking for anything: if they see the right image, they put their heads there. Sometimes they put their heads between the mare's forelegs, sometimes between the hind. At some point they hit an udder bursting with milk. Wriggling their lips, they sooner or later find a teat in their mouth, and reflex sucking takes over. This splendid reward shapes the searching behaviour, making clear that some pairs of legs have teats and milk while others do not. After a couple of days they have learned which are valid and make no more mistakes.

The foal's reaction, then, shows the same pattern as that of the herring gull chicks' gaping at Tinbergen's stick with a red dot: both animals react to a drastically simplified but exact symbol, not their entire mothers. Innate releasing stimuli (also called releasing stimuli, trigger stimuli or sign-stimuli) and programmed responses (fixed action patterns and the like) can suffer the same problems as insects' automatic reactions: the response may not be such a good survival ploy when the animal meets with unusual conditions that fortuitously provide the basic characteristics of a releasing stimulus. Wagtails can spend hours fighting their reflections in car wing mirrors. I once went to sleep in a Colorado forest and was woken by the purr of a humming bird's wings next to my ear. It was making as if to feed from the red letters on the book I had laid down: humming birds feed from red flowers. A newborn foal I was watching repeatedly put his head between a tree and a gatepost linked by a heavy bar: two uprights capped by a shadow. He ignored his mother.

During the whole magnificent sweep of evolution, of animals, plants, bacteria and viruses inventing new ways to solve the problems of surviving, there have been some consistent trends if we look at newcomers. Evolution is blind: it does not lead anywhere except survival and procreation. There is no endpoint to be arrived at, no apex or pinnacle, but a continuous flux and adjustment to continually changing conditions. Nonetheless, if we consider new life designs in the long history of living beings, there is a consistent trend towards less wastage. Huge numbers of insects die because they cannot modify their innate reactions in inappropriate circumstances, like moths attracted to candle flames. In terms of behaviour, less automatism and more ability to react to a complex of stimuli, not just one outstanding feature, mean fewer suicidal or silly time-wasting mistakes. Decisions can be made as to whether or not to act, or how exactly to do it. In mammals, increasing brain size and ability to analyse and consider situations means that innate reactions are less fixed: not so often is there an automatic reaction to an innate releasing stimulus, as a tendency to find certain stimuli curiously

*Fig. 1.2   Many simple behaviour patterns have an innate base but are perfected by experience. Standing with their necks overlapping comes naturally to these foals, but what comes next is not so obvious. With practice they will mutually groom more efficiently. (Photo: Javier Solis)*

attractive, fumble about a bit and, partly by chance, discover that one way of behaving brings unexpected satisfaction. Next time, the fumbling about diminishes and the animal is more goal-oriented: it now knows there is a goal, instead of being driven by a vague compulsion. Innate reactions provide the conditions for learning.

The formula S → R is a simple way to say that a particular stimulus provokes a particular response. In innate behaviour, the link between the two is, so to speak, ready-made in the animal's mind. In learned behaviour, the link is forged or changes in response to the animal's experience of the consequences of its actions.

## LEARNING

Learning takes many different forms that, in the field, are often mixed so that what is going on is not clear. For this reason its investigation took place in the laboratory where the conditions could be simplified and controlled. Nevertheless we mostly see the same features in animals' natural lives once we know what we are looking for. The foal's learning how to get food is an interaction between innate and learned behaviour and reflex action.

The simplest form of learning, shown even by animals that have no brain at all, is habituation: losing a response to a stimulus that normally provokes it. Horses are particularly prone to fear any moving thing that has not been proven safe, but after a few startle responses that have no consequences except a waste of energy running away, they habituate, or 'get used to it'. You cannot spend your life running away from butterflies or rabbits, though foals start by doing so. Like most young mammals, foals are helped to distinguish between what is genuinely dangerous and what is not by their mothers' attitudes.

Investigation is a kind of self-programmed habituation. After removing himself to a safe distance, the horse returns cautiously to the unknown thing, watching and listening, ready to flee again if it reacts adversely. If there are no consequences, he finally gets near enough to examine it with all his other senses – smell, whiskers, lips, teeth, feet – to identify it for further reference.

In associative learning, a new S→R link is forged. Classical conditioning links a new stimulus, previously irrelevant, to an already existing response. Thus horses learn to neigh at the sound of our car. Operant conditioning forms a new response, a new behaviour. Horses also learn to be remarkably adept at opening stable doors. What forge and strengthen the S→R link are reinforcement and repetition.

Reinforcement can be positive or negative. Positive reinforcement is usually called 'reward', which makes us think of food. True, food is powerful reinforcer, especially when an animal is hungry. It makes the animal repeat whatever was done before to get it. But any pleasant feeling, like being in good company for a social animal, is reinforcing. So is habit, or repetition.

Negative reinforcement involves an animal finding itself uncomfortable and, as a result of its reactions, becoming comfortable again. The second time round, it is quicker to repeat what it did previously. Thus positive reinforcement involves something pleasant being added, while negative reinforcement involves something unpleasant being taken away. In training horses, negative reinforcement is widely (and by some trainers exclusively) used: pressure and release. A moment's thought shows that it is not a particularly pleasant way of learning: the horse would prefer not to be made uncomfortable in the first place. He learns just as fast as with positive reinforcement, but is not motivated to 'go to class'. Rewards, on the other hand, do motivate, for any animal is eager to be rewarded. Once he has learned what to do to get a reward, he keeps performing even when he is not rewarded, although occasional rewards keep both motivation and performance at a high level.

*Fig. 1.3   Investigation or gradual, free-choice habituation: the youngsters lose their fear reaction by exposing themselves to the stimulus.*

A bunch of feral horses find a distant tree with rich fruit in autumn. After finishing it they wander back to their normal grazing area, to return to the tree (*operant conditioning*: they have learned the way) occasionally but fruitlessly throughout the year. In autumn they are rewarded again (*infrequent rewards keep them performing*). In time they may connect the tree's fruiting with the appearance of blackberries in the area they normally graze (*classical conditioning*), and cut down on their fruitless visits. As the years pass, the tree is simply where this bunch goes in autumn, a cultural habit.

Punishment, or unpleasant or frightening experience, is capable of temporarily suppressing a reaction, but not of destroying an S→R link: sooner or later the animal will revert to its previous response and keep doing so unless punished again, or rewarded for behaving differently (counter-conditioning). Punishment cannot create a link; it provokes fear of the situation in which it occurred. In horses, punishment provokes avoidance, their usual reaction to a fearful situation. With repeated punishment a horse recognizes, and takes evasive action at, the preliminary signals that the situation will recur: avoidance learning.

To return to the example above: the farmer, enraged, protects his fruit tree with an electric fence. The horses, punished, learn to recognize and avoid it at first sight, though they still return every autumn. Satisfied, the farmer stops electrifying the fence. Sooner or later the horses revert to touching it, find it does not hurt and push through, for which they are rewarded.

Avoidance learning is the secret of success of threat, which is followed by attack (punishment) if ignored. Finally, one animal may avoid the mere approach of another even without threat: passive displacement.

Punishment, like reinforcement, can be positive or negative. Positive punishment is the infliction of pain, discomfort, anything disagreeable. Negative punishment is the removal of something desirable. Since horses desire company, being chased away by others is a form of negative punishment.[1]

Discrimination learning involves differentiating between a valid stimulus, one that brings reinforcement if you respond, and one that doesn't. Horses discriminate carefully between hundreds of different types of plant, just by feel. As foals, they nibble tiny samples of plants. Poisonous plants generally taste bad, but the foal does not eat enough to poison himself: he is merely sampling, learning to connect the feel of the plant to his whiskers and lips with a good or bad taste. Later, he will flip aside the bad ones with impressive speed and certainty, using that wonderfully mobile upper lip, as he grazes.

## COGNITIVE PROCESSES

Beyond the level of pure connectivism or behaviourism are cognitive processes: the collection and recollection of information, together with its analysis and integration, to form concepts and make decisions. Horses, dogs, chimps and most notably humans are capable of examining situations and considering possible outcomes before acting appropriately rather than simply reacting to cues, whether learned or innate, though we do not always use this ability. It makes us curious. We like information for its own sake, not necessarily with some immediate purpose in mind but because knowing how the world works satisfies an innate urge.

Horses are naturally inquisitive and exploratory. Most domestic horses, though, have little opportunity to investigate, explore, or reach their own conclusions and decisions, for they are too restricted and controlled. Like other animals, horses learn to learn; if they are brought up in dull, unvarying environments, repeating the same mindless exercises, they have little chance to learn and do not strike us as being bright. As the Italian ethologist Francisco de Giorgio insists, limiting our training to behaviourist control techniques annihilates their cognitive abilities and their satisfaction in using them.

One of horses' particular talents is that of making mental maps of where they have been; it includes the ability to predict how known places or routes link up with each other without ever having explored the link before. This is cognitive learning without reinforcement or punishment. It is seldom allowed to develop, but horsemen who work in difficult terrain – on mountains where thick mist descends suddenly, in dense, monotonous scrub or confusing forests – know and treasure this ability, unconsciously fostering it by allowing the horse more freedom of choice in picking his way than would a dressage rider.

Are horses capable of forming concepts? Experiments show that they learn concepts like always choosing the bigger (or smaller or darker) of two images on a screen, but the best examples are in working horses, cowponies, logging horses, general farmwork horses and the like, who show that they genuinely understand their work despite its huge variability. Their introduction to it is usually via stimulus/response learning, but after a period of confusion and unwillingness, most grasp the idea of what is to be done, do it eagerly and even invent ways of resolving tricky situations without any prompting. A behaviourist might say that this is simply avoidance learning (*I can feel he wants me to move so if I do so now I'll avoid getting kicked*), but avoidance learning does not produce eagerness. Many years ago I met a logging horse, quite alone, manoeuvring a huge tree trunk down a steep wooded slope. Whenever it snagged, he made careful tests to feel and calculate angles before throwing his full weight in precisely the right direction to free it. Fascinated, I followed him down; if I offered suggestions he told me to mind my own business, which at that point was realizing how appallingly dull normal training is for them. They like using their cognitive abilities.

Mammals with brains as highly developed as horses have an enormous capacity for learning, which allows them to adjust to the particular conditions they find themselves in. They retain reflexes that deal with simple reactions, automatically controlled patterns like gaits and, especially for the newborn to help them through their first days of life, innate responses of the type described by Tinbergen in birds. But they have shifted the control of most of their behaviour from automatic to formed-by-experience, though what pushed them into the experiences was often an innate urge. Horses, being social animals, seek company, an innate urge that nonetheless does not provide them with the knowledge of how to behave once they find it. In a natural life, a foal learns to distinguish between individuals, to communicate by recognizing and using signals, to respect others' individual space, to know how to invite another to play and make friends. He sees his father sexually aroused and mating, sees newborn foals, and death, too. All happens so gradually and smoothly that we do not realize what a wealth of learning social life requires and supplies. Domestic horses who have grown up without company are often social inadequates, creating havoc in the company they so yearn for; young mares are often terrified by a stallion's display, and some are scared of those weird, wobbly, unhorse-like foals they produce. They are ignorant, through no fault of their own.

## TINBERGEN'S FOUR TYPES OF QUESTION

When we watch animals going about their everyday lives in their natural habitats, the core business of ethology, we do so with the aim of describing first of all what they do and then finding out how, why and what factors influence it. To find that this behaviour is innate, learned or produced by an interplay of the two is to look at the way it is produced, the *how*. It does not answer *why* the animal should behave that way. Tinbergen, who had a particular, fierce clarity about framing questions so that they might have concrete answers, saw that the answers to 'why?' questions fell into four groups. This classification has been a lasting help to ethologists in framing their questions.[2]

## 1. Proximate Cause

What was it that triggered this behaviour? The trigger might be a stimulus, a situation, a rise of a certain hormone that makes certain stimuli more interesting, or a bodily state, like being cold. The stimulus might be innately recognized or become significant because of experience; the reaction may be innate or learned or, most often, an inextricable mixture of the two. A proximate cause is what provoked the behaviour.

## 2. Final Cause

How does this specific behaviour affect the animal's chances of surviving and breeding successfully? What are the long-term effects of such reactions on its life, or the survival of its offspring? Final causes may be stunningly obvious – eating keeps you alive – or may be difficult to tease out. Stallions urinate on their mares' dung, which might seem to convey a message of 'she's spoken for' to another male finding it, who smells it carefully; he then

*Fig. 1.4    Smelling his mare's dung, this stallion detects she is in season by doing Flehmen. He then sprinkles the dung with urine, thus neutralizing the telltale pheromone. (Photo: Javier Solis)*

performs Flehmen, raising his head and rolling his upper lip back over his nostrils to prevent air escaping, pumping it into the vomeronasal organ within the nose. This organ is specialized in the detection of pheromones, smell-messages that change the hormones, and thus the behaviour, of the animal who detects them. An in-season mare's dung contains such a pheromone that sexually excites a male, who rushes off to find the mare. Kimura (2001) noticed that when, marking his mare's dung with urine, a stallion does not urinate in the usual jet, which would suffice to tell others of her alliance, but sprinkles it over the dung in a peculiar way. On collecting and analysing samples, Kimura found that the stallion's urine neutralizes the mare's pheromone: by sprinkling the dung all over with urine the stallion maximizes its neutralizing effect and fools would-be competitors. Now we know the final cause, even if he does not.

## 3. Development

Some behaviour is appropriate at one stage in life, some at another. Newborn mammals suckle by reflex; adults do not. Young female animals do not produce full sexual behaviour: they do not have the resources to complete their own development into healthy adults and produce offspring at the same time. Animals are by and large parsimonious in the invention of new behaviour, so that what has been an appropriate reaction at one stage may be taken over for another use at a later stage. What has been play becomes courtship; what has been a wolf cub's begging for its mother to regurgitate food becomes symbolic allegiance to the pack leader. I had a pet starling who, before fledging, gaped vertically when I offered food. At fledging, he gaped horizontally, so I had to drop the food in front of him. Little by little he directed his bill-opening downwards, often missing the food entirely; a couple of weeks later he would stroll around the field, point his bill downwards and open it, the way that adult starlings discover insects hidden among grass. It was not until I saw the full adult behaviour that I realized what the clumsy transition phase was about.

## 4. Evolution

Selection, whether natural or artificial (i.e. by us) clearly shapes innate, genetically determined behaviour. Sometimes the same behavioural habits are developed as a result of different selection pressures. Foxes do not behave like rabbits, although both dig holes and sleep in them.

   Social living has evolved in many different animal groups, but may have different benefits according to the animals' way of life. Most carnivores are not social. Those that are usually hunt in coordinated packs, like wolves, orca or the little African wild dog *Lycaon*. Sometimes this enables them to take prey much bigger than they could alone. Many of the animals they prey on, like caribou, seals and zebra, also live in groups, but for wholly different reasons: for them, there is safety in numbers. Others group for other reasons. Red deer form groups in the mating season, with fierce competition between stags for control of the groups of does. Social living can be the answer to a variety of problems. We should not, then, assume that all animal societies are organized along the same lines. Social relations will vary according to the particular benefit deriving from group living.[3] By studying the natural selection pressures that operate on the animal, its evolutionary development, we can see how the different patterns of social behaviour evolved to confer different benefits.

In the next chapter we will examine the horse's evolutionary history to see what selection pressures drove the shape of the equine body and behaviour.

Particularly deep-rooted is an animal's defence behaviour in the face of life-or-death situations, for there is no time for learning or fumbling about until a satisfactory solution arises. Whatever an animal's chosen ploy in order to save its life – leap into water, climb a tree, shoot down a burrow or run away – it must follow instantaneously, automatically, when danger threatens. In turn its selected defence reaction shapes other innate behaviour. If water, tree or burrow are essential to the survival plan, avoid straying too far from them; if running away is the plan, better not sleep in enclosed places.

The innateness of patterns of defence behaviour does not mean that animals cannot learn to discriminate between different threatening stimuli and to habituate to some but not others. An animal's learning ability, too, is shaped by its evolution: not only in terms of whether it can learn at all, but what it can learn readily. With their rich social life, horses are quick to distinguish and remember individuals (as well as plants) and to learn to respond to signals, even ones made or invented by us. They are not quick at learning to recognize triangles or do the Spanish walk. Evolution has shaped the mind so that some S→R connections are easily, almost invariably, made while others take a great deal of effort to connect, if at all. It has also shaped their cognitive processes: a major consideration in horses' decision-making is safety, whereas a wolf's is more likely to be affected by the chances of making a kill.

## MOTIVATION

Often when we ask 'why did the animal do that?' we mean 'what made it want to?' or 'what motivated it?' This is a tricky question.

What we now call motivation was once called 'drive', which perhaps better describes the feeling we have when motivated, as if driven to do something. Enormous efforts were made to produce an overall theory of drive, but it became so convoluted, still without fitting all the facts, that it collapsed, though not before provoking years of argument, definitions and re-definitions. Like the word instinct after the collapse of Lorenz's model, drive was replaced by a hitherto neutral word without history.

There is no general theory of motivation. Each case is taken on its own merits, though there are groupings, behaviours that seem to work in the same way. Consider the flow diagram, borrowed from systems analysis, which seems to fit many cases of maintenance behaviour well:

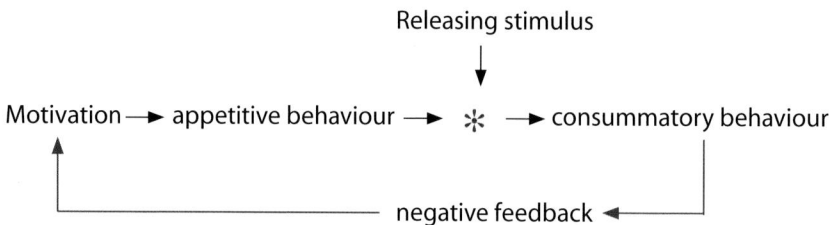

Releasing stimulus
↓
Motivation ➝ appetitive behaviour ➝ ✳ ➝ consummatory behaviour
↑ │
└──────────────────── negative feedback ◄──────┘

Or: an animal gets hungry (is motivated to eat). It goes out looking for food (appetitive behaviour). When it finds some (releasing stimulus), it eats (consummatory behaviour), and no longer feels hungry (negative feedback). If it is very hungry, it may accept food that it would not normally eat (stimulus generalization).

In this case, motivation increases with time. In some cases it may not. A mare comes into season and looks for a stallion, but if she does not find one she does not, as it were, get hungrier and hungrier. After a few days her motivation will disappear anyway, being under hormonal control. Motivation often is, even hunger.

But what drives a social animal to seek company? We do not know. What we do know is that when appetitive behaviour driven by innate motivation cannot find a releasing stimulus because the animal is not in its natural environment, it is liable to repeat bits of it in an obsessive way, in stereotypical behaviour. Stabled horses, deprived of freedom, company and grazing, are prone to develop senseless, repetitive habits, even to the extent that they damage themselves; abruptly weaned foals are likely to suck the manger in a frustrated attempt to find the security of the udder. These habits accompany changed levels of neurotransmitters and hormones that alter the animal's whole physiological and mental equilibrium: the animal is stressed. Yet how the original levels of these substances made the animal want to seek company, liberty or the mother, we do not know; nor can we switch off motivation genetically encoded during millions of years of evolution, except by putting the animal in circumstances nearer those for which it is adapted.

## STRATEGIES, COSTS AND BENEFITS

Even with the same motivation, animals of one species, especially if they are mammals, do not always gain their ends in the same way. John Maynard Smith, a mathematician who turned to population genetics and then to behaviour, was a man with an extremely lively mind, who

*Fig. 1.5    As they graze, horses advance one foot, eat around it, advance the other foot and sway to eat round it: a pattern that is reproduced in stereotypic weaving in stabled horses without access to grazing. (Photo: Javier Solis)*

loved playing with ideas. Naturally, he was attracted by games theory, which points out that, in card games for instance, there is often no single winning ploy. People have different strategies for winning, often changing them as they work out what the other's strategy is. Maynard Smith applied this to different genetic alleles controlling behaviour in his theoretical hawks and doves model, in which the names do not represent different species but different ways of behaving. In conflicts, hawks are always aggressive and kill their opponents. Doves never fight. You might think that the population would end up being all-hawk, but as the proportion of hawks rises so that they meet more often, so does the carnage they inflict on each other, while the doves live together peacefully. The population finally reaches equilibrium long before all the doves are killed off. By adjusting the relative advantages of the two ploys (for instance hawks may always kill doves but only maim each other, or doves succeed in escaping sometimes) different proportions of hawks and doves are present at equilibrium.

Games theory gave ethology a new slant. Do animals like horses have different strategies, different solutions to life's problems? They do. For instance some stallions are more aggressive than others, flying to attack any other male they see. This might give them an advantage if there were something to be gained, like first chance at a desert water hole that many bands have to share. But when there is nothing to gain, aggression has no advantages, and distinct risks of getting hurt as well as the disruption it causes to others in the band. Peaceful stallions who avoid fights have more and better foals, for peace is necessary for small foals to feed and rest enough.

The benefits (gains) and costs (risks) of different strategies may, as in the example given above, differ according to the exact conditions in which the animal lives. Games theory gives us a way of calculating how the environment shapes behaviour. It also gives us an insight into how experience shapes behavioural strategies. When animals gain something by fighting, they are more convinced of the value of fighting next time; when they lose and get hurt, they are more likely to avoid fighting. These 'winner effects' and 'loser effects' are a key to the behaviour of domestic animals forced to compete for food, when some get more and more aggressive while others grow more and more timid.

## EMOTION

Emotion often provides a powerful source of motivation, as we know only too well. To what extent are we justified in thinking that animals have emotions like ourselves? Here lies an immense, but diminishing, gap between the attitudes of the scientist and the animal keeper, a gap that had its roots in Descartes (1596–1650).

Descartes was an extraordinary, brilliant, rational thinker who left us a tremendous legacy: the definition of the scientific method, the fallibility of philosophizing about the natural world without considering evidence as did the Platonic tradition, the basis of coordinate geometry and more. But not all his ideas were so great, and the not-so-great ones influenced Western thought as much as did the brilliant insights. One was the dichotomy of body and mind, or what his Jesuit training led him to understand as a human soul. Only recently are we coming to the conclusion that the two cannot be divided. Another was that animals are entirely mechanical, having no soul, Therefore, he supposed, they were incapable of feelings or emotions.

For hundreds of years Descartes' views dominated science. Animals were not considered to experience emotions: they 'exhibited aversive reactions' but did not feel fear or pain. Although Darwin had no doubt that animal emotions are highly adaptive, the scientific world continued experimenting on animals as if their physical and emotional suffering did not exist. Only very recently have Marc Bekoff and Jane Goodall launched a serious attack on this attitude.[6] Both are renowned ethologists, but both waited until they were no longer dependent on scientific grants to publicize their conclusions: that the emotional centres of the brain in humans and many highly developed mammals are so alike in form and function that the subjective feeling of emotions in animals cannot be denied. The tardiness of formulating these views is underlined by work like that of Harlow in the 1950s on the effects of maternal deprivation on monkeys,[7] which contributed enormously to our understanding of the factors contributing to emotional problems typical of neglected children; or that of Joe leDoux on fear, which used rats to elucidate what happens to traumatized people and how to deal with it.[8] If what animals experience emotionally parallels our experience, then it does. Their fear and pain are no different from ours.[9]

But we must also be careful here. Because mammals like horses and dogs have the neural centres for, and seem to show and be motivated by, emotions like fear and anger does not mean that they also feel pride, embarrassment, ambition, guilt, duty, or a moral sense of right and wrong. Although this latter group of feelings may motivate us as strongly as the first, people show huge individual and cultural differences in just how strongly they feel them and what they attach them to. They are learned feelings that depend on our particular society or upbringing. Many depend on our peculiar ability to imagine how others are judging us. There is no evidence that animals have it.

One of science's great guiding principles is Occam's razor, so-called after the philosopher William of Occam (1280–1349): 'entities should not be multiplied without necessity'. Or: do not invent new factors to explain events unless you have to. A corollary is: if you do have to invent a new factor, it should explain more events than the one that made you invent it. Newton's idea of gravity did; Lorenz's model of instinct did not. A later psychological formulation of Occam's razor, Lloyd Morgan's principle (1903), states 'on no account should behaviour be attributed to a higher psychological faculty when a lower one will do'. Or: do not imagine that newborn foal is searching for milk if his behaviour can be explained by a ready-made S→R connection. Keep your explanations as simple as possible.

## ANTHROPOMORPHISM

We have such immensely sophisticated brains, incorporating such ideas as ego, foreseeing the results of our plans, and imagining what others are thinking, that we do not realize just how sophisticated these ideas are. Until we have proof that animals have these ideas, we had better believe that they do not.

Anthropomorphism is a word with a strange evolution. In ancient Greece it meant thinking that gods were driven by the same desires as men: Greek gods were rather wont to be carried away by lust, jealousy, fury and ambition. Nowadays anthropomorphism means thinking that animals behave for the same reasons as we do, a pitfall that traps many animal lovers into mistreating their pets, albeit unwittingly. One of our most fixed misconceptions is the idea that animals have a sense of right and wrong in the same way that we do. 'He knows he's done wrong' says the dog-owner on coming home to a trashed house, 'look at his guilty face'. Applied ethologists spend their time and patience explaining that the dog fears the furious look on the owner's face, for he has learned it means a beating. Beatings, however often repeated, do not teach dogs not to feel distraught when abandoned. Moral right and wrong are human concepts that animals lack; what they do appreciate is whether an experience is pleasant or disagreeable, so that we can teach them, by manipulating rewards, that what we want them to do is pleasant for them. A more cognitive approach is to allow the animal to explore, in its own time and way, a situation that we have set up and draw its own conclusions. In equestrian terms, 'fix it up so the horse can find it', as the trainer Ray Hunt put it.

To what extent, then, can we assume that animals have feelings as we do? Is seeing and empathizing with an animal's pain or fear a kind of unjustified anthropomorphism, or a justified, scientifically based reaction? From neurological studies and observation, there seem to be basic emotions that more advanced mammals do share with us: fear, pain, joy, curiosity, surprise, anger and disgust.[10] (I would also add affection, or bonding, often mediated through the hormone oxytocin; but scientists have a curious antipathy to using words like affection or love when referring to animals – though Harlow did.) What they do not share are the emotions that we feel because of our society or culture: pride, embarrassment, the moral sense of right and wrong, the sense of achievement, duty, *schadenfreude*. As we know only too well, these vary both between individuals and between cultures.

## APPLIED ETHOLOGY

Applied ethology deals with the behaviour of animals in our hands, in particular with the problems they find in adjusting to unnatural lifestyles and to our expectations of them.

Although wild animals of the same species can and do adjust their behaviour according to their exact environment or their individual strategy, cost/benefit analysis shows that these adjustments are adaptive and fall within a range of 'normal' behaviour for that species. An ethogram is a dictionary of such behaviour, often the result of innate motivation creating situations in which the animal learns to behave appropriately for its species. When an animal is kept in conditions well outside the limits of what it would meet naturally, its innate motivation may be permanently thwarted; appropriate learning situations may not arise, or rather inappropriate behaviour may be fortuitously reinforced. Stress, the result of being asked for more adjustment than the animal can make, alters its hormones and neurotransmitters, making it particularly prone to obsessive behaviour and inability to learn. Any of these factors, or a combination of them, can give rise to aberrant behaviour; behaviour that is neither adaptive in the circumstances in which the animal finds itself nor seen in wild or feral animals.

The applied ethologist's task of finding out what is causing the behaviour and alleviating it is usually complicated by owners' anthropomorphism. Many people have difficulties grasping the fact that animals do not have any concept of right and wrong or of what they 'should' or 'should not' do. Others, who have bought an animal to serve a particular purpose, cannot conceive that the animal does not feel a duty to perform: to work, that is, to repeat actions at the owner's whim; to put up with conditions far from those for which its evolution has prepared it, or to please us because we feed it. Many seem to imagine that when animals irritate, hurt, embarrass or frustrate us they do so quite deliberately and maliciously. We have complicated imaginations.

When we consider how and why horses evolved as they did, the reasons for horses' behaviour become much clearer and simpler.

## CHAPTER 2

# What Horse Evolution Can Tell Us

Fossils are not the best material for studying behaviour, but they can give an expert a wealth of clues about how an animal lived and moved. When we find a series of fossils showing a consistent trend, they can also indicate what were the main selection pressures as this evolutionary line of exploration adapted to new environments.

When we look at a branching evolutionary tree, with its lines that die out and others that give rise to animals living today, we are liable to forget that what seems to be the end point – now – is not a fixed one. The world changes continuously. What may have been satisfactory solutions for living on land fifty million years ago are not likely to be so fine today. Continents

Million years ago

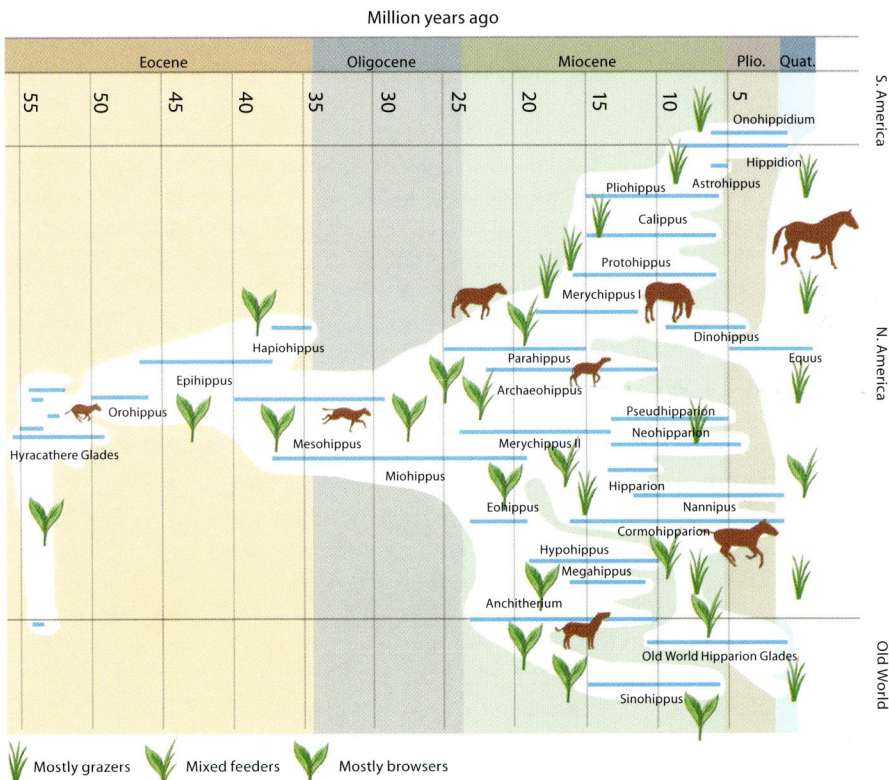

*Fig. 2.1    Horse evolution, from McFadden. During the Miocene there were many species of proto-horses, varying in size and adaptations as they struggled with the problems of new habitats…and predators. But at the end of the Miocene, 5 million years ago, most became extinct. Others hung on until the end of the Ice Ages, 12,000 years ago, when they became extinct in the Americas and much of Europe.*

float about and collide, changing ocean currents and land masses so the climate changes. The animals and plants that make up the surrounding ecosystem adjust and change, too. And so, of course, do natural selection pressures.

Fifty million years ago, well after the dinosaurs disappeared, the world was not as it is now, but warmer and steamier, with less temperature difference between the equator and the poles. Large sections of it were what we would call tropical or subtropical forest, and grass did not exist. North America was not attached to South America but formed a huge continent with Europe and Siberia.

## EARLY FOREBEARS

The first of the line that later gave rise to horses, *Hyracotherium*, flourished at this time. It was no more like a horse than the contemporary little proto-monkeys were like modern man. Hyracotherium was the size of a hare, scampering flat on its four-toed feet in the forest, where it browsed on leaves and fruits. Its eyes faced obliquely forwards and its brain was small. Nothing is known about its habits, but it was small enough to dash for cover when attacked. Some of its probable predators were the two-metre high 'terror birds', Phorusrhacidae, whose huge slashing beaks could make mincemeat of little *Hyracotherium*.

During the next twenty million years, slightly different forms of the same creature arose, although they showed no major changes. They had toes, they never grew to more than 50kg, they lived in forests eating leaves and do not seem to have been very bright. Modern tapirs, although bigger, are the latest form.

But the world changes. North America split from Europe and became joined to South America by a land bridge, cutting off a great ocean current and provoking a profound climate change. The world became cooler and drier, the poles colder. As the forests shrunk in extent, new kinds of plants, grasses, appeared and covered increasing stretches of land. While some of the forest dwellers stayed in the forest, experimenting with adaptations to cope with the changes, others ventured out into this brave new world.

## GRASS AND PRAIRIE DWELLING

Grass is not an easy source of food. It is hard, requiring good grinding teeth to mash it up. Its high content of silica, the main element of glass, makes it so abrasive that teeth wear out quickly unless they grow constantly and are specially protected. Having folds of harder enamel winding through dentine, the softer main component of the tooth, means that, as the tooth wears, these folds survive as hard ridges standing above the worn dentine. The effect is like that of a rasp, an efficient way to shred grass. The group of perissodactyls (ungulates or hoofed mammals with an odd number of toes, like horses and zebra – artirodactyls like pigs and cows have even numbers of toes) that took to the savannahs and prairies increasingly perfected this new type of tooth. Some species stayed eating forest leaves; others became grazer-browsers; some lines went back and forth between the two. Around twenty million years ago there was an astonishingly wide variety of proto-horse-like creatures inhabiting slightly different ecological niches, or even coexisting in the same ones, in North America. They also crossed the land bridge and invaded South America.

Grass has another disadvantage as food. Unlike leaves, which can be mashed up into a nutritious soup, grass is often mainly stem, composed of cells with hard walls and little rich content. Indeed, its main nutritive value is in the cell walls, made of cellulose. Unfortunately, animals lack the enzyme to break down or digest cellulose into more usable components. On the other hand there are types of bacteria that are excellent at the job. Grazing animals harbour huge colonies of these bacteria in their guts, a symbiotic relationship in which the host animal profits from the broken-down cellulose while the bacteria profit from a sheltered, perfect environment in which to multiply. Horses use the caecum as the bacterial harbour; ruminants use a chamber of the multiple stomach.

What fossils cannot tell us about is the evolutionary struggle to provide a perfect environment for useful bacteria while avoiding breeding harmful ones. A delicate balance must be found.

To offset its disadvantages, grass offers some strong advantages as food. On the prairie it is everywhere, and does not move. It does not need trapping or stalking. Tool-making is unnecessary, forward planning eliminated. Horses are extremely carefree about the future availability of food. If, when they live in enclosures, we give them too much hay, they eat what they need at the moment and, in their carefree way, destroy the rest by strolling about on it, lying on it, defecating and urinating on it. Their habits are not adapted to resources that are scarce and valuable, as a dog's are: if we give a dog too much food he eats what he needs and hoards the rest for later. For a dog (or us), food is hard to come by; for a horse, it is as easily available as air. Like air, it does not provoke competition: it may be of better or worse quality, but since it does not come in rich, discrete lumps as does meat, it is not worth fighting over. Conflicts over who is to have control over it are senseless. We would not expect horses to be territorial: apart from the lack of concept of control, the time and energy spent in patrolling the limits of a territory big enough would not leave enough time for eating.

The necessity of attacking and killing other animals for food is also eliminated. Predatory behaviour is not, in fact, aggressive (although you might be forgiven for thinking so if attacked by a tiger): it involves different neural circuits to those involved in aggression. But a grazer's life does not involve predatory interest in other animals.

## PHYSICAL DEVELOPMENT

The shift to the prairie was accompanied by other changes. *Hyracotherium* and its descendants ran on four toes, though they increasingly diminished the fourth to run on three. Little by little the central toe became the main weight-bearer, with the side toes as props like the little side wheels on a child's first bicycle. Stubby nails like hippopotamus's became hoofs, especially on the central toe. Until the end of the Miocene, five million years ago, horses ran on three toes. Some crossed the Bering Straits from the Americas and colonized the Old World.

They also grew bigger. One advantage of being bigger is that it makes you harder to kill. There is a great deal of evidence to show that these plains-dwellers' lives became increasingly influenced by the menace of predators evolving to feast on their rich, grass-fed flesh. Their eyes gradually shifted to the sides, giving a wider visual field. Their legs changed in proportion, elongating the light, muscle-free metacarpals that form the lower leg and concentrating the heavy locomotor muscles higher in the body. The effect was to create a block moving along on light, long-striding legs, an energy-efficient way of covering ground fast: the peasants of the Landes in southern France did the same, effortlessly striding about at high speed on stilts. In comparison a lion has not reduced the weight of its lower leg or elongated the metacarpals; it achieves stride length and speed by arching its spine, a technique that soon exhausts it, whereas a horse can run full tilt for several kilometres without slackening speed. The impact of the weight on the lower joints was gradually absorbed by the development of the suspensory ligament, a spring that also gives effortless lift-off in the next stride. The neck became longer, an effective counterbalance allowing longer stride and recovery of balance in the suspensory phase of the gallop.

All in all, these changes meant increased perception of approaching danger, faster geta-way and a greater capacity for sustained speed. They were necessary. The Miocene was also a period of carnivore expansion. *Smilodon*, the tremendous sabre-tooth cat, weighed up to 200kg; it appeared in the Miocene and continued to terrorize proto-horses until the Ice Ages. Huge bear dogs (amphicyonids) took their toll too.

At the same time, the proto-horse fossils show a great increase in brain size, especially of the neocortex. The neocortex performs many functions: sensory analysis, integration and what we would generally regard as intelligent, rather than automatic, behaviour. Robin Dunbar, an evolutionary primatologist, has shown that, in primates, neocortex size is linked to social living or, more precisely, to the size of the group and the number of relationships this entails.[11] Social interactions require learning, considerations and decisions – neocortical specialities. In ungulates, neocortex size does not follow group size so much as the complexity of social interactions: some ungulates, like wildebeest, live in large groups without seeming to mind exactly who is in them or having individual relationships; others, like horses, live in smaller, stable groups with highly developed individual relationships.[12]

Dunbar's 'social brain' hypothesis suggests that the shift to the prairies prompted proto-horses into complex social living at the same time as they found themselves engaged in an interminable 'arms race' against predators. Was that coincidence? Or did social life help them in their struggle?

The majority of the varied forms of perissodactyls dwindled and died out at the end of the Miocene, for reasons that are not completely understood. Possibly they were outcompeted by ruminants, which took rather longer to evolve their complex, but highly efficient, digestive system. Horses, with their small, simple stomachs, have to graze almost continuously: sixteen or eighteen hours daily. With their heads down and the jaws working noisily, they can be surprised by predators. Ruminants graze fast, filling a storage stomach and later regurgitating the food to digest it. They can avoid grazing at dangerous times when predators are on the prowl, dawn and dusk. Ruminant digestion took longer to perfect but is more efficient than equids'. Moreover, ruminants have evolved all kinds of headgear, horns, antlers and the like, which they often use for sexual display but can be handy for defence, too. Some, like prong-horn antelope and goats, actually attack predators. Equids are far more vulnerable. Perhaps that is why there are only seven species of equid – two horses, asses, onagers and three types of zebra – and around 150 of ruminants. The equid design has its disadvantages.

Nevertheless some lines of the three-toes did continue until around three million years ago, when the climate changed again, becoming even cooler. It was to get colder still as the Ice Ages followed, eliminating most of these survivors until only the lines we have today remained. During this time horses became more definitely horses as we know them, reducing the two side toes to mere vestiges, the splint bones, and forming a splendid single hoof. Interestingly, this was not done by losing the genetic information about how to form side toes, but by suppressing it. Occasionally a horse is still born today with three toes if the suppression is not complete.

Although the whole story of horse evolution was concentrated in the Americas, horses could and did cross the bridge of the Bering Straits, spreading across Siberia into Europe.[13]

We do not know when, where or how the modern horse *Equus caballus* came into being.

It is not a descendent of *E. przewalskii*, the Asiatic wild horse, although they seem to have shared a common ancestor over 50,000 years ago. What we do know is that at the end of the last Ice Age, around 12,000 years ago, horses became extinct in America and northern Europe. Przewalski's retreated to the Mongolian steppes, but various races of *E. caballus* survived in the Iberian peninsula. The Portuguese marsh Sorraia, the *marismeño* from the Doñana in southern Spain, and the Basque mountain pottoka have DNA that can be traced back at least to the last Ice Age.

## EARLY DOMESTICATION

The first proven domestication of the horse was in the steppes north of the Black Sea and in Kazakhstan, around 6,000 years ago. By then, cows, goats and sheep had been domesticated for around 4,000 years and pigs for 3,000; dogs, which seem to have domesticated themselves from wolves by hanging around inhabited caves (Kipling got that right), for as long as 30,000 years. Why did it take so much longer to domesticate horses? Their meat and milk are more digestible than most ruminants'.

The answer may be geographic; but it may also lie in their behaviour. Ruminants wander off grazing, leaving their youngsters to sleep soundly and opening the possibility for a watchful hunter to locate and steal one. If the mother returned furiously, the hunter had supper, too. Mares never leave their foals, but guard them while they sleep. Stallions also protect foals. Foal-stealing is not easy. The first horses to have been captured seem to have been young males in bachelor bands, whose natural boldness and curiosity may have led them to be trapped more easily than the more cautious breeding animals.

Domestication has various consistent effects. It means altering an animal's lifestyle, forcing it willy-nilly into a new ecological niche. Even within the same species, animals vary in their adaptability: some will not thrive, though those with less acute reactions to stress do. The process of domestication selects only certain stress-tolerant individuals.

Secondly, we want animals that are easy to handle: calm, gentle, forgiving ones. Aggressive ones get eaten first and do not live to breed. Stupid animals, those that do not mind our inconsistencies, suit us better than intelligent ones that learn from a single experience. Domestication reduces brain size, usually by about 10 per cent, though in pigs by as much as 30 per cent (Kruska 1988).

Thirdly, we breed from already domesticated animals: taming wild animals is hard work, often dangerous and disappointing. Once a mare has been secured, her young foals tame easily.

The combination of these effects means that the wide genetic variation typical of wild populations is drastically reduced in domestic populations, which are, on the whole, less intelligent and have less severe reactions to stress. Domestic races, becoming inbred, are often outcrossed to other domestic races, increasing their genetic variability, but the original selection leaves its marks on the DNA in what is called a genetic bottleneck. Such bottlenecks can also occur when a population has been reduced to only a few individuals. The entire extant population of Przewalski's horse derives from nine horses; some native breeds, like the Exmoor and Asturcón ponies, became almost extinct before being revived, so that their genetic pool is extremely limited. While the resulting morphological uniformity pleases us, we do not know to what extent their genetically controlled behaviour also suffers from a bottleneck effect. To judge from feral horses, who take to the wild like ducks to water and have successfully colonized small islands, high mountains, deserts and marshes, not a great deal.

The innate reactions of domestic horses to anything they perceive as threatening, the legacy of their evolution as prey animals, are still our greatest problem with them.

What the present-day horse's evolution suggests is that the two great selection pressures that shaped the horse's body – eating grass and not getting eaten by predators – will have shaped the behaviour too. A reasonable hypothesis is that their ancient habit of living an intense social life will reflect both these evolutionary trends, in the lack of competition for basic resources and in their necessity for behavioural defence against predators.

Is that what studies of feral horses show us?

## CHAPTER 3

# Equine Ethology Studies

Ethology is the study of the behaviour of wild animals in their natural habitat. While there are vast numbers of 'wild' horses living without any management or interference all over the world (except in tropical forests, tsetse-fly savannah and the icy poles), they are, almost without exception, not bred from original wild populations but from domestic horses that escaped to breed as if wild. They are feral.

Equine ethology got off to a slow start. Ethologists were prejudiced against studying escaped domestic animals, even those that had faced and survived the same problems as true wild species for generations. Curiously, the pitfalls of studying wild animals in captivity did not seem so obvious. Wolves, baboons and chimps in zoos were studied, and influential conclusions drawn from their behaviour. More recently, as the behaviour of wild wolves, baboons and chimps has been observed in great detail, the contrast between their behaviour and that of those in captivity has made clear that captive animals suffer behavioural and social stress that alters their behaviour, and that such altered behaviour is not natural but a consequence of unnatural conditions amounting to poor welfare. The behaviour of once-domesticated feral animals becomes the key to understanding why their still-domesticated counterparts, whose innate motivation and specific learning abilities are so adaptive in the wild, often appear stupid or even self-destructive, and show stress-related behaviour when, to our eyes, they are well cared for. For the horseman, the study of feral horse behaviour is the basis for understanding why domestic horses behave as they do and whether we are treating them appropriately.

## EARLY STUDIES

The first overall study of horse behaviour was made in 1972 by Stephanie Tyler on free-living New Forest ponies. Strictly speaking, these are not feral: there are few stallions, which often do not live year-round with the mares, and once a year colt foals are removed. In winter they are fed hay that, being in piles, creates competition (so do the titbits offered by tourists, and the goody-laden garbage they leave behind). Win-lose relationships between the competitors become established. While many of Tyler's observations correspond perfectly with those on true feral horses – how horses divide up their day in bouts of grazing, followed by resting, followed by moving; how they roll, get rid of flies, signal anger or bonding (affiliative) behaviour; how they court, copulate, raise their foals, and how their foals gradually become independent – her observations on social relations often do not. The relative absence of males and the competitive relationships change the social dynamics within the groups.

## Feral Horse Bands[14]

When studies on true feral populations began, the behaviour of males when they comprise about half the population became clear. In 1976 Feist and McCullough published what is now a classic study on mustangs in the Pryor Mountains, Wyoming. They found that feral horses do not live alone but in bands, of two main types: natal bands and bachelor bands.

Natal bands are breeding units. Usually they have one, sometimes two or more, stallions; an average of three to five mares, though some, especially the two-stallion bands, have many more and others less; and youngsters up to around two years old, or sexual maturity. They then leave the band and join another. This natal dispersal, as it is termed, minimizes the chances of inbreeding, and both sexes do it.

The colts join the second type of band, the all-male bachelor band, where they stay until they acquire mares and form their own new natal bands.

Occasionally mixed bands of immature youngsters are found wandering, not attached to any main band; these mixed-sex peer groups, as they are called, are not invariably seen as are natal and bachelor bands.

The studies that followed confirmed these groupings as the general rule in feral horses. Pelligrini studied mustangs in Nevada, Salter and Hudson those in the high Rockies of Alberta, Miller those in the baking Red Desert of Wyoming; Berger slithered up and down the vertical desert of the Grand Canyon before doing an immensely valuable five-year continuous study in the Great Basin of Nevada, where 2,600m mountains surround a basin that dries considerably in the summer. Patrick Duncan and others including Claudia Feh studied a marshland herd of Camargue ponies originally without any management, though in recent years the population has grown to the extent that management is essential. Welsh observed a population of ponies on Sable Island, a small sandy island in the middle of the North Atlantic where sheer starvation was the commonest cause of death. Some island populations derive from shipwrecks, others from deliberate abandonment by sailors. A line of off-shore sandbank islands along the eastern seaboard of the United States, Chincoteague, Assateague, Shackleford Banks and the Rachel Carson Sanctuary are home to feral ponies who have been the subject of many studies, for they are quite tame, easily observed and easily accessible, in contrast to remote mustangs and brumbies, who tend to be wary of mankind. Additionally, there have been Japanese studies of Misaki Island ponies, studies of New Zealand horses who share their range with Army manoeuvres, and studies of Asturcón and Gallego ponies in the Spanish mountains: we now have many studies on feral horses.

As results accumulated they sometimes seemed to vary widely, which barely seemed surprising given the range of variables. Not all horses termed feral live without any management. Some, like Tyler's, are rounded up every autumn (the drift) and foals, especially colts, are taken off, leaving one stallion to twenty or thirty mares (Chincoteague, Asturias, Galicia). Some studies are very much more intensive, careful or long-term than others; reports from local people may suffer from imaginative interpretation; students with a thesis to produce may know their ethology and statistics but lack familiarity with aspects of equine behaviour, or be so familiar with them that habitual interpretation colours their observation.

Results and conclusions, then, may disagree because of genuine population differences that reflect adaptations to different environments, or because of differences in maintenance, method, terms and interpretations: human factors. Linklater (2000) summarized the results of nineteen studies including ones on zebra and showed that the differences were not because of the horses but down to human factors. (Reader, be warned: do not be satisfied with reading the précis of conclusions presented in an abstract on the Internet. Read the entire paper and note how the study was done.)

Linklater's conclusion was that feral horses all over the world, no matter what their racial origins or the wide variations in their habitats – desert, marsh, high mountain, tiny over-crowded island, rangeland, savannah – always have the same basic organization: they live in polygynous breeding bands, practice natal dispersal, and non-breeding males live together. Neither type of band is territorial, although they do have home ranges. Where the stallion/mare ratio is low as a result of management, the stallions have natal bands and the surplus mares wander alone with their offspring, or in little bands. When they come into season these mares smell out a stallion, present themselves for covering, and go off again.

Such a system evidently has deep innate roots, not modified by environmental circumstances.

## DEFINITIONS AND DESCRIPTIONS

Since definitions of terms we use are important to avoid such confusions, here are some I use in this book (but note that others may not make the same distinctions).

## Grouping and Living Associations of Horses

- **A band** is a number of feral or free-living horses living together by free choice, for months or years.
- **A group** is a number of domestic horses living together not by choice but because we have put them together. Their living space is much reduced and they are often hand-fed, so the influences on their social behaviour are more like those of zoo animals than of wild ones.
- **Feral horses** are those having no management at all – except, obviously, exclusion from the best grazing areas, reserved for cows – mustangs (USA), brumbies (Australia), cimarrons (South America), baguales (Patagonia) and the like. Assateague, the site of numerous studies, had such a problem with over-population that some mares are given long-term contraceptive injections that prevent them from breeding during several years. Treated mares tend to change bands often, disrupting band stability (Nuñez et al. 2009)[15]. The island is popular with tourists so the ponies are often hand-fed or petted, or fight over garbage. So although always considered a mainstay of feral horse studies, Assateague ponies do actually have a good deal of human influence.
- **Free-living horses** have some management that changes social relations, like a reduced number of stallions as a consequence of colt culling, or winter feed, but they are free to choose their social associates: Chincoteague, New Forest, Asturias, Galicia; native ponies and meat horses bred free-ranging on the hill; the Tour du Valat herd in the Camargue.
- **A home range** is a non-defended territory in which a band lives. Home ranges have *core areas* where the band spends at least 50 per cent of its time, and outlying areas they visit regularly. Occasionally, every few months or so, they may make exploratory expeditions further afield.

However, natal bands are remarkably loyal to their core areas. Even when they make annual migrations up mountains to escape the heat and flies below, they will return to the same area for the rest of the year. Linklater shows that this loyalty mainly relates to the stallion. At one end of Shackleford Banks the stallions are more loyal to, and more defensive of, their core areas than to the mares, who tend to wander to and fro. Whether this is true territorial behaviour is a moot point, for it lacks other characteristics of territorial behaviour. In fact all mares, on changing bands, change home ranges too.

Home ranges overlap, especially in richer pasture or round water, which creates opportunity for band changes. Natal band home ranges vary from 25sq km in poor conditions like deserts, to 0.2sq km on overcrowded islands. Bigger bands have bigger home ranges. Bachelor band ranges are very much larger, for they go round exploring and spying on natal bands, endlessly seeking mares: one might be wandering, a filly might be ready for natal dispersal, a stallion might be getting old and careless.

## Natal Band Members and Characteristics

Natal bands are often popularly called harems, a misleading term since it seems to imply that one stallion has absolute control over the mares. Firstly, natal bands in all populations sometimes have two or more stallions, not just one. Secondly, although natal bands are fairly stable – the most stable breeding groups seen in ungulates – mares can and do change bands if they want. Especially when young, they may take time to settle into one band. Older mares are usually more loyal to one stallion (or is it home range?). Depending on the population, up to 30 per cent of mares choose to change bands in a year, and the stallion cannot stop them if they are bent on leaving. He does not control them, but is their consort.

A band is a band because it stays separate from other bands; its members move from one maintenance activity to another as a unit, eating, resting (these two together occupy some 90 per cent of their time) and marching together to new pasture or water.

*Fig. 3.1    The stallion's usual position is on the outskirts of the band, and he places himself between the band and any threat or unusual occurrence – such as a keen photographer. Pottokas, Spain.*

*Fig. 3.2    When herding, the stallion adopts an unmistakeable posture. Although his flat ears and wrinkled nostrils show annoyance, he is retrieving this youngster into the safety of the band, not driving it away. (Photo: Javier Solis)*

### Stallions

Stallions are the bands' protectors, dealing with outside menaces like predators, other bands or marauding bachelors. They are the mares' bodyguards, paid with the right to have foals. Naturally, they defend both their breeding rights and their foals.

On the march, the stallion usually comes last, where he can see that all are present. Grazing or resting, he generally occupies a peripheral position. He spends far more time in vigilance than the mares who, often pregnant and lactating, must spend more time eating than he (Duncan and Boys). Rifa, who clarified the stallion's role in Asturcón ponies predated by wolves, saw that the mares attend to his attitude and actions if danger threatens, when he places himself between the band and the threat. He may lead or herd them away from danger. In herding, he lowers his head and, with flattened ears, wobbles it on an outstretched neck, an unmistakeable sign that all those of his band move away from. He also uses this posture to herd straying members back into the band, or to group or move the band when other males are near.

The stallion tends to regard the proximity of other males to his mares as a threat, but how close is too close? Studies are annoyingly vague about this question, though one does mention that bands are never less than a hundred metres apart. In my experience it depends on the population, the circumstances, the time of year, and even the individual stallions. In the Snowy Mountains, the brumbies I spent two intensive weeks studying were always kilometres apart, never within sight of each other. On small, flat overcrowded islands this is impossible. On the *páramo* of Cotopaxi (Ecuador), at a breathless 4,200m, many feral bands grazed peacefully side by side on a rare area of good grazing, about 8 hectares, giving the impression of a

Fig. 3.3 Two fused bands on Cotopaxi whose members intermingle. A third band (left) is very close but separate. (Photo: Javier Solis)

Fig. 3.4 After smelling each other, these two stallions display furiously, squealing, stamping their forefeet and arching their necks. (Photo: Javier Solis)

large herd fluctuating as bands came and went. Only careful scrutiny revealed that each band seldom mingled with another but left a no-man's-land of some twenty metres between it and the next. Since members of the same band could be twenty metres apart, the first impression was of a homogeneously scattered herd. Newly arriving bands took up peripheral positions and gradually worked their way in to the better grazing without any conflict. Berger also mentions bands grazing together without any conflict. On these occasions the youngsters wander and greet those from other bands, although the mares do not. This allows the youngsters some idea of where to go at natal dispersal. In winter or a non-breeding season stallions are more relaxed about proximity and mare defence.

When bands do meet unexpectedly, for instance on the march, the stallions usually stop and stare, then rush headlong towards each other. Stallions and mares look similar, and judging from their keen expressions both stallions are hoping the other is a mare. They meet, sniff noses carefully, then move to smelling the withers, then under the belly. Both shriek with horror: it's male! At worst, there is a brief, intense explosion of rearing, pawing and biting at each other. Joel Berger, who watched 499 such clashes in Nevada mustangs, says that most lasted less than thirty seconds and that in 98.5 per cent of cases there was no clear winner. At best, this phase consists of furious stamps with the foreleg and indignant squeals. Deciding not to have a real fight, the stallions try to out-impress each other, arching their necks, stamping and performing passage, the high, lovely trot they also use to impress mares. In particular they do passage in parallel, as if seeing who can bounce highest. Finally they settle down to the Great Dung Pile Ritual.

One stallion, with a pompous air, smells the ground, moves forward and defecates where he has smelled, turns and smells his product and retires a few metres. The second comes forward, smells the dung and, lifting his feet high so as not to contaminate them with the offensive matter, steps over it and dungs on top. He turns and smells the pile and, satisfied that his smell prevails, retires a few metres. The first returns, smells the combined pile, steps over it, dungs on top, turns to smell it, retires. The second stallion steps forward, smells… This goes on until neither has any dung left; their last efforts are the size of peas. The whole ritual is performed with an air of such immense solemnity that you can recognize it kilometres away. Then they both go back to their mares.

This frankly absurd-looking performance gives both stallions the chance of relating the smell of dung with a particular character whose strength and fighting ability have been tested in the brief clash. Rubenstein and Hack showed that stallions can recognize each other from the smell of their dung. Neither wants to fight, but a wise stallion profits from knowing what might happen if the other wanted to, for instance if a wandering mare were in season. Along the sides of paths in areas common to several bands, stallions use common dung piles, smelling the last contribution carefully before adding their own and smelling the result, so that each knows who has gone before. A stallion might decide that another was only a few minutes away and turn his mares back by herding them.

Rubenstein has also shown that, in the rather special conditions of Assateague, where grazing is so limited that starvation was the major cause of death and good grazing is limited to small patches, weaker stallions recognize stronger ones and move their bands away if stronger ones arrive. A stronger stallion, then, is able to benefit his foals, through their mothers' getting better grass whenever they want to. Not unnaturally, mares tend to choose these stronger stallions. However, no such similar effect has been shown in other populations without those special limiting conditions, although home ranges do vary in quality and, as a result, the production of foals.

Bachelors (*see below*) rarely get greeted or honoured by the stallions' meeting ritual.

*Figs. 3.5a and 3.5b    Ritual dunging. The two stallions take turns in smelling and dunging on each other's dung. (Photos: Javier Solis)*

Stallions tend to fly at them instantly, biting their sides and rumps as they flee. Sometimes, though, a stallion does greet one and even play a little with him. Berger, whose long-term study enabled him to know each horse's paternity and history to an extent that others cannot, saw that the bachelor was likely to be the stallion's son, now embarked on a new life stage.

*Mares*
Mares dedicate their lives to raising foals, safe in the knowledge that the stallion's vigilance protects them from danger. Although they may prefer to graze alongside one mare rather than another, they do not form the exaggerated friendships seen in domestic horses. Nor do they mutually groom with other adult mares, though they do with the stallion, their foals and, often, yearlings (Granqvist *et al.*).

There is no indication that they compete for grass. When grazing is scarce they spread out, avoiding competition. As this generally coincides with the non-breeding season the stallions are more relaxed about letting the mares further away: an opportunity for band change, or for an alert bachelor to steal one. When water is scarce and they are thirsty, they push and shove to get at it first.

Mares do, however, protect band stability by trying to eject any mare who comes to join them, a move that may be countered by the stallion's herding her back in again. Eventually they will allow her beside them and finally to integrate into the band. Stable bands have better breeding success than unstable ones; so do the bands of stallions that avoid conflicts. Loyal mares who do not change bands breed better, too. Small foals suckle up to four times an hour, so disruption easily disturbs their feeding. When the mare is not in the best of condition anyway, as is often the case in feral horses, disruptions can cause a foal's weakness or even death. The more peaceful and stable a band is, the better its breeding rate. Domestic horses also try to protect group stability by rejecting newcomers, and quiet, friendly newcomers are accepted more readily than nervous or conflictive ones.

# Natal Dispersal

When a filly first comes into season, she is attracted by her father's smell and solicits him, often in a rather puzzled way, raising her tail, urinating frequently and 'winking' her vulva. He steadfastly ignores her; he may even become irritated by her misplaced attentions and drive her away. Finally she makes off to find another male. Since males can detect the smell of an in-season mare from kilometres away, possibly there are some around. Sometimes the filly, after mating, returns to her natal band (and mother) and does not leave until the next year, but these young mares have less chance of breeding a healthy foal than those who settle rapidly into a new band. The stallion's habit of allowing his fillies to fraternize with others when bands are close would seem to be a help.

Stallions do not seem to have a magical way of knowing their own daughters. Their rule is not to mate with a filly who has been born and grown up within the band. If the stallion has acquired a mare already pregnant by another stallion, or a bachelor has sneak-mated one in his band, he will not mate with her daughter. Conversely, if he has lost a pregnant mare and meets her daughter later, he will happily mate with her. So the mechanism does not always avoid inbreeding, though mostly it does. Similarly, mares will not allow colts from within the band to mate with them, but refuse them furiously.[16]

*The bachelor band*

Colts leave of their own accord at between two and four years old, without any aggression from their fathers, and join a bachelor band. A bachelor band comprises males without mares, mostly up to around seven or eight years old and, sometimes, old ones who have lost their mares. They have a great deal of fun play-fighting together, investigating anything that catches their fancy, and harassing natal band stallions. They try to steal mares, to sneak-mate, to track lost mares: a carefree life of developing strength, agility and fighting skills, of learning about potential danger and deft use of social signals, and *cherchez la femme*.

## Bachelor to Stallion

Most bachelors do not achieve mating until six years old or so, and most cannot maintain a natal band until seven or eight. When they are younger and acquire mares they generally lose them: they simply do not seem to be serious or attentive enough. Mostly they acquire mares without fighting: by being on the alert for a filly in natal dispersal; by stealing a mare from an inattentive stallion, or in thick woods or brush; by finding a mare separated from her band while giving birth … opportunities arise for those who keep their eyes open. But if the years pass and a bachelor has not had any luck, he may decide to battle a resident stallion for his band. His frequent play-fighting leaves a bachelor able to assess his ability: younger bachelors do not attempt head-on battles but limit themselves to trying to steal mares.

Such older bachelors have often already assumed a stallion role in the bachelor band, herding the others, taking lookout duty and the major defence role; they may then spend time living alone. As testosterone levels rise with maturity, the bachelor becomes more single-minded in his search for mares: persistence is one of the characteristics of testosterone.

*Fig. 3.6    A bachelor band watches the stallion Lazan. On the left, Elegante and Bambino, whom we saw later as stallions. The pale dun is Padrote. On the right, Mechas, who died of piroplasmosis three years later.*

Battles are furious, frightful, and may result in lethal injuries for either participant, so they are not undertaken lightly. The moves, of course, are the same as in play-fighting: rearing and lunging to knock the other off his feet, biting at the jugular or biting behind the elbow so the other drops to his knees, then biting the tendons. Ears are vulnerable, and so are flat back. The resident, especially, as he chases the intruder, is likely to get his teeth or jaw broken by a well-aimed kick. There may be repeated sessions. But in the end, the bachelor, if he has chosen the right opponent, wins.

Immediately he chases the mares away furiously, biting them, or may force-mate them. This produces abortion if the mare is less than five months pregnant, though not later. Although the mare does not necessarily come into season again after aborting, and indeed rarely produces a foal until well over a year after take-over, the new stallion has at least eliminated his rival's offspring (Berger).

Recently a great deal of attention has been paid to reports of stallions killing foals, especially colt foals. The first, which came from what had been regarded as a wholly feral herd in the Camargue, shocked those of us who look at feral horses until, on closer reading, it turned out that the stallions concerned had been confined during the winter and suddenly released among mares. (Reader beware: *read the small print*.) Foal-killing has not been seen in feral horses and is not a part of normal behaviour; nor has it been seen when stallions live permanently with mares, only when stallions are released with mares and small foals after having been confined, usually all winter. Even then it is rare. Horses are not lions.

However he has acquired his mares, a stallion's behaviour changes as soon as he has them. He no longer seeks out mares – although if they decide to join him he welcomes them – but occupies himself with defending those he has to the best of his ability.

### Multi-stallion natal bands

These are more common in some populations than others, but are seen in all. Miller showed that, in the Red Desert where water sources are extremely scarce and bands may have to queue up to use them, large bands automatically jump the queue and drink first. As two-stallion bands are often bigger than single-stallion ones, they have an advantage.

The relations between two stallions in a band vary. In one form, one stallion does not let the other mate at all, while the second defends the band against other males, and dangers. The costs for the second seem to outweigh by far the benefits, but he is allowed to mate and remove the first stallion's daughters to form his own natal band, so he seems to be playing a waiting game. Another version is that of two weak stallions who travel together, each respecting the other's right to breed with his own mares. A third is that of two firm bachelor friends

*Fig. 3.7   A two-stallion band on Cotopaxi. Brillante (resting, far left) kept close to the mares while NegB, here on guard duty, dealt with external affairs. (Photo: Javier Solis)*

who, having acquired mares together, share them. Whatever the arrangement, these bands are not as stable as single-stallion bands and tend to break up after months, or few years. An argument developed between Feh (the Camargue herd), who sees them as genuine alliances that benefit both partners, and Linklater (New Zealand Kaimanawa horses), who sees them as an uncomfortable temporary truce that is readily abandoned.[17]

## HYPOTHESES

The hypotheses raised by our rapid rush through equine evolution were that:

a)  horses have an intense and complex social life in which
b)  competition for control over resources is non-existent or minimal;
c)  defence against predators is paramount and affects social relations.

These hypotheses are partially, but not wholly, confirmed by extant studies, which have not necessarily been looking at behaviour from that point of view.

Are horses social? They certainly are, compulsively so. Compared to other ungulates their bands are small and stable, and they have intricate individual relationships with others in the band.

Is there any sign of within-band resource competition, that is, between the members of the same band? In the matter of eating, none: as far as possible they avoid competition, though they are not above a bit of shoving when eager to drink.

In extreme conditions, competition between bands is sometimes seen, as in Miller's water-hole access study, where size of band wins, or Rubenstein's, where bands with strong stallions gain preferential access to small patches of good grass. Rubenstein denies within-band competition even in this case.

However, the polygynous mating system, that of having various mares to one stallion, does of course provoke competition. Maximizing the number of foals, which is the stallion's preoccupation, is related to, though not wholly dependent on, impregnating the maximum number of mares. Maximizing the number of healthy live foals also depends on ensuring that their mothers are well fed and that predators do not eat them. Home range quality affects fertility, foal growth and survival; it may also affect the mare's choice of stallion, if the stallion is the one most loyal to the range. What determines which stallion has which home range has not been addressed, since they do not defend their ranges; nor has the question of why they have home ranges at all.

While horses who already consort with mares do not compete between themselves for more, bachelors clearly do compete to acquire mares. At first they adopt the strategy of trying to sneak-mate, but gradually change to that of permanent associations. How they choose a home range of good quality, one that raises strong foals and attracts other mares, is not known, for no studies, even Berger's, are sufficiently long-term to follow a bachelor's history until he is a mature stallion with years of foal production behind him. Whether one stallion is more inherently attractive to mares than another, or what makes him so, has also not been investigated, though Asa and others showed that, given the choice, free-living stallions tend to prefer mature mares. They are more reliable breeders.

In fact the huge question of why horses have such a mating system, the basis of their social lives, has not been considered. Ungulates in general are notorious for having many different mating systems, which fall into two main groups (Isvaran 2005). One is female defence, when a male defends the female against others; it includes long-term or seasonal pairing, harems, grouped female defence as in horses, defending one in a large mixed-sex herd like buffalo, or temporary defence of a willing female found by wandering about (roving). The other is resource defence, when the male defends some attractive place and the female comes to him, as in various forms of territoriality and lekking (males displaying competitively for females). Most ungulates switch strategies fairly easily according to varying circumstances, like population density or resource availability. Horses do not. Apart from sneak-mating as younger bachelors, they stick rigidly to their natal band system, with only the slight variation of having multi-male bands sometimes. Why? With so many options open to them, this one must have some advantage for them.

As for our third question, that of defence against predators, there are no studies at all. What they do in the face of attack, how defence affects social relations, whether the mating system is in itself an adaptation to defence, whether the home range system is connected in any way: a host of questions arise from the consideration that the horse's primary natural selection pressure seems to have been predator danger. They have not been examined.

## MY OWN STUDIES

Lucky to have spent my graduate and postgraduate years among many eminent ethologists and heard their arguments in development, I nevertheless tired of academic life and its constraints and returned to the land of my fathers, the Welsh mountains. Taming and training 'wild' Welsh ponies raised on the hill gradually brought home the connection between academic ethology and practical horse training, although in those early years only Tyler's study had come out. Efforts to develop training methods that sidestep the normal resistances, difficulties and accidents involved in horse-breaking pointed inexorably to ethology as the key. Yet equine ethology, although fascinating as it developed and often supplying hard scientific fact to firm up my suspicions, failed to give me answers to the questions that beset me, including ones that had no immediate practical application but were simply paths to understanding the horse.

If you deal with horses raised in freedom, or badly treated ones, you cannot help but be impressed by their terror and paranoia. How do they deal with that in the wild, where dangers are real?

So began a search for free-living and feral horses anywhere I could find them: native ponies on the hill raised in semi-feral groups; mustangs in Arizona, brumbies in the Snowies, cimarrons in Venezuela, criollos on Cotopaxi, baguales in Patagonia and the feral herd of pottokas I set up in Spain.

My tools are my eyes, binoculars, a notebook, a stopwatch and a counter: none of the sophisticated methods of data collection and analysis that professional scientists now enjoy. On the other hand I am blissfully free of the 'publish or perish' pressure they suffer, able to take a wide-angle view and let the questions present themselves rather than extend some established line of research. I encourage my students to do the same: to absorb the overall picture before them, make meticulous observations on whatever catches their eye and allow the questions to emerge and be tested with due rigorousness, rather than to base their questions on previous research.

Nevertheless these observations have crystallized into the coherent, logical picture of social behaviour that, for me, was lacking.

Most of the following chapters concerns two populations in particular that I know well for years: feral criollos, or cimarrons as they are called locally, in the *llanos* (flatlands) of Venezuela; and pottokas, Basque ponies, that I released on a Spanish mountain in 2008 to live without any management. Effectively they are feral. I describe both in detail here.

## The Venezuelan Cimarrons

Cimarron is a term widely used in South America for feral horses, while criollo refers to a race bred in and adapted to local conditions. In many countries, like Argentina, Paraguay, Chile, Brazil and Venezuela, domestic criollos largely derive from the re-domestication of cimarrons. These cimarrons in turn descended from escaped horses brought by conquistadors and early settlers, so their original blood or mixture of bloods varied, as does the racial type of criollos from different countries.

Venezuelan cimarrons appear to derive exclusively from Spanish blood. The first horses brought by Colombus were not the magnificent Andalusian chargers he had bought but, as a result of a nifty last-minute switch by dealers who did not think he would come back, rather ratty little horses from the Doñana marshes, the marisma. These *marismeños*, whose origin is unknown but may well be genuine wild horses, still live free on the immense, treeless delta of the Guadalquivir, where the pitiless heat and mosquitoes of the summer are matched by the freezing winds, driving rain and flooded marshes of the winter. Even today, natural selection is fierce. They are immensely tough little horses.

Colombus left his on the island of Hispaniola (Dominican Republic), where they bred and were used for later expeditions by conquistadors. Although DNA testing has yet to be done, Venezuelan criollos bear a closer resemblance to *marismeños* than to any other Spanish breed: straight-backed, droop-rumped, with a low-set tail. The head is straight, occasionally sub-convex. They, too, are immensely tough little horses, around 140cm, agile and tireless.

The cimarron population greatly increased during Bolivar's War of Independence (1811–27) when, inevitably, rather a lot of people fell off or let horses loose. At one time there was an estimated population of 300,000. As settlers came, their numbers decreased. In the *llanos*, the vast flood-plain of the Orinoco and its tributaries that extends some 500 kilometres north into Venezuela and an equal distance south into Colombia, cimarrons held their own until relatively recently. Ranchers threw many kilometres of fence across the plain, finding they had enclosed whole herds that they gradually diminished. The herd we studied is one of these. As far as we know, it is the last big (150) herd of completely unmanaged cimarrons, though there is said to be one equally big in Colombia.

Hato los Camorucos is a typical *llanos* ranch, 11,000 hectares ring-fenced in the 1920s by the Vargas family, enclosing thousands of capybara, caimans and turtles, rather fewer deer, giant anteaters, puma, jaguar and anaconda, and 300 cimarrons. The herd was split into two. One half (the 'tame' herd) lives on improved pasture; the horses are branded, wormed and vaccinated and the colts broken to use as cowponies. The other half was left without any management. Until our arrival in 2007, a bachelor band was caught some years to make up numbers for work, but since then the tame herd has provided enough saddle horses. In 2000, internal fencing cut down the cimarrons' original range to 1,200 hectares. Dr Vargas, a vet, says that this does not seem to have affected their behaviour except in the winter: they used to move to another part of the farm, which they can no longer do. They share this enclosure with between 400 and 800 cattle, mostly Brahma, so that depending on the time of year they are disturbed by the *llaneros* (cowboys) rounding up cattle. This has actually proved useful for my studies on stampede behaviour.

*Fig. 3.8    Cimarron mares grazing among Brahma cattle, los Camorucos. The grey mare standing sideways had advanced trypanosomiasis, and died later. She also had melanomas, which a caricari scavenger bird is cleaning here, so she probably had maggots too.*

The climate is extreme. There are two seasons. The dry, hot summer lasts from November to late April; with midday temperatures up to 40 °C, the land becomes parched. Winter starts with violent thunderstorms that gradually settle to constant rain. By June the River Apure, a tributary of the Orinoco, bursts its banks, flooding the flat land to a depth of a metre or so with filthy water, in which the horses live and graze. From the constant immersion the ends of their tails rot, so that all have tails the length of a normal yearling's. Winter brings plagues of mosquitoes, tabanids and other biting flies, carrying trypanosoma, a blood parasite similar to malaria, from which most of the horses suffer. The *llaneros* say that, at times, there are so many flies and mosquitoes that all the horses look black. Infectious anaemia is also endemic. Outbreaks of lethal encephalitis, brought by migrating birds, are uncommon but devastating. There was no outbreak during the time of our studies (2007–11) but in 2011, a plague of ticks brought Babesia (pyroplasmosis), which killed a fifth of the herd.

Curiously, the nearest European equivalent to these conditions is found in the Doñana marisma, the horses' probable site of origin.

The horses suffer from predation by puma and jaguar at near-natural levels. The massive neighbouring Hato el Frío (80,000 hectares) was, until 2011, a nature reserve. In Hato los Camorucos puma are tolerated unless they prey heavily on the calves near to the ranch: one was killed only half a kilometre from the ranch installations in 2011 after despatching six calves. The cimarrons' enclosure began some six kilometres further away. We often found puma trail and faeces, and early-rising students spotted them slinking about their business in the pre-dawn light. At 70kg or so, puma are too small to kill an adult horse unless the horse is already dying, but they do prey on foals. Typically, they open the back of the skull after peeling the skin forward over the face, and lick out the brain. Puma hunt in open savannah, unlike jaguar, much bigger and more powerful, that stay in the wooded areas. We did not identify jaguar kill (perhaps from ignorance; they are said to crush the skull).

The cimarrons' enclosure is roughly square, mostly open savannah, and absolutely flat. At about a third of the distance between the south and north fences, a raised bank runs west-east. Some three metres high, it stands clear of the winter floods, so that clumps of trees can grow on it. From the west, these clumps are Flor Amarillo, Flor Blanco and The Camoruco, according to our nomenclature. Rather charmingly, the *llaneros* call these '*montes*' or mountains. They are linked by a raised track (*terraplen*) along which maintenance vehicles sometimes pass. We call it the cordillera (the mountain chain). Further east are scattered acacia bushes grading into solid head-high scrub. Finally, at the extreme east there are tall trees, which to the north-east surround a lagoon. Some of these trees, like the ceiba and the saman, are leguminous, and have rich pods upon which the horses feed.

On the north side a side-branch of the river winds into the enclosure at one point. It dries into a series of pools in the summer, but there is never a shortage of water.

The flat savannah is grass, with patches of low, prickly acacia.

This bald description does nothing to convey the magic of the *llanos*. The absolute flatness

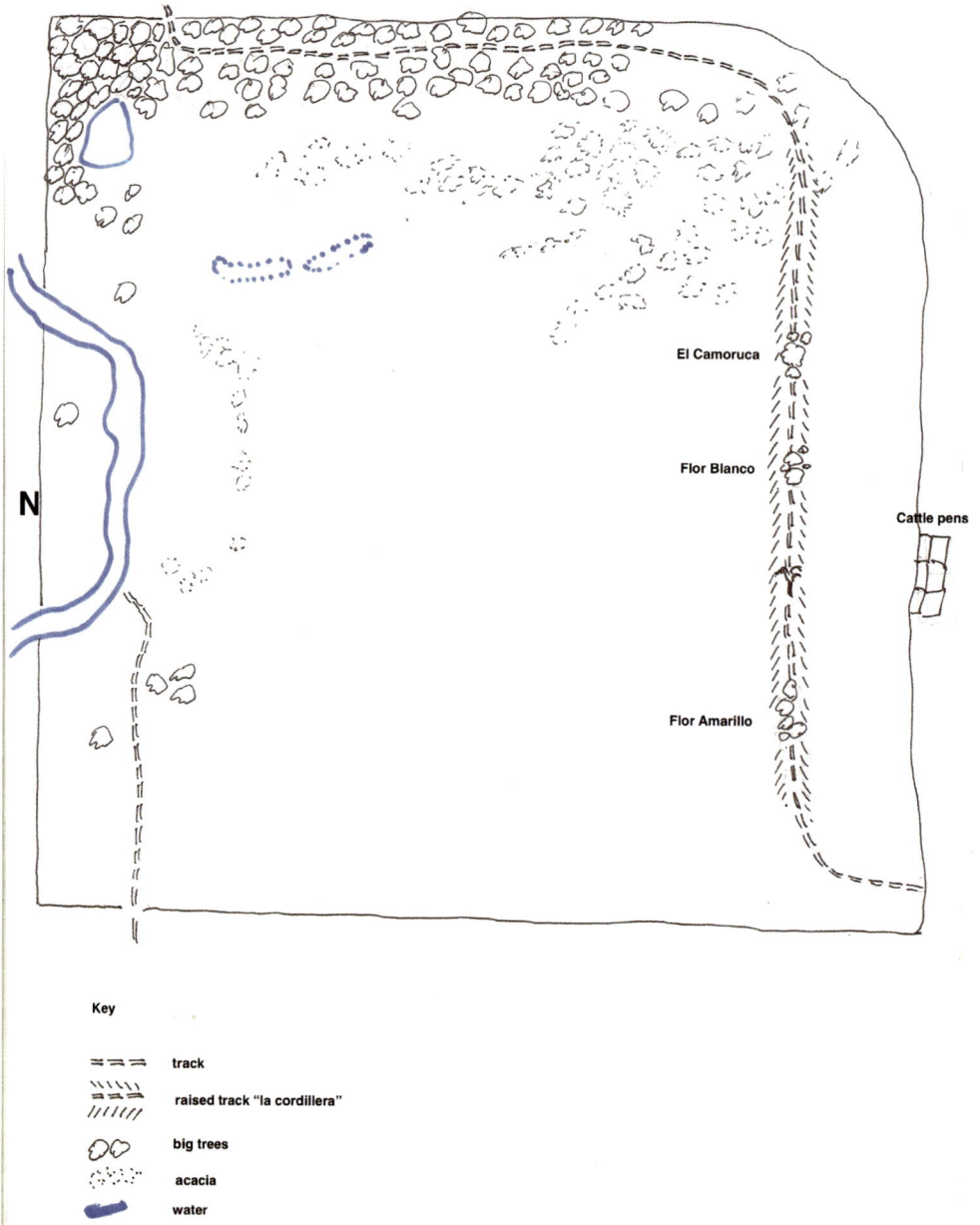

El Camoruca

Flor Blanco

N

Cattle pens

Flor Amarillo

Key

≡≡≡   track

\\\\\\
≡≡≡   raised track "la cordillera"
//////

○○   big trees

acacia

water

*Fig. 3.9   A sketch map of the cimarrons' enclosure, Hato los Camorucos.*

of the land makes the sky immense, so that you seem to be walking in an infinity of time and space.

My studies began in 2007, when Vanesa Ugarte, my friend and assistant, and I were invited to visit this typical *llanos* ranch, and spent ten days zooming out on a quad before dawn to search out the horses and spend all the baking day watching them. Although the sight of a mounted *llanero* some kilometres away stampeded them, the horses had never seen people on foot, so they were wary and curious rather than terrified by us. With binoculars, observation was easy in the clear air of the open savannah.

For the next four years, I ran residential ethology courses in the Hato. We stayed during the whole of April. It is the end of the dry season and, around the twentieth, the first thunderstorms begin, so we saw the savannah change from brown to green, literally overnight, the lovely *llanos* lilies spring up, and clouds of migrating birds move in. April is the end of the foaling season, when coverings and births are frequent, the most interesting time to watch a herd. Also, the mangoes on the great trees around the house ripen, so the howler monkeys, the scarlet macaws in their raucous pairs, the capybaras, iguanas, tortoises, butterflies, horses, cows and mules shared our enthusiasm for the new season's fruit.

The horses became well used to us on foot and we could sit 50m away without causing any disturbance, offering easy observation with binoculars. Until the rains came, we observed for four hours daily, from dawn until 10a.m., when the heat becomes unbearable. After the first rain, it was cooler and our hours varied.

Every year we spent one or two nights camping out in the savannah to see what happened at dusk and dawn.

Skeletons and dead bodies were aged by their teeth. I did not know whether to assume that the wear of the teeth in these horses is the same as that of domestic horses kept at pasture, but during a veterinary exercise I correctly aged twenty working horses in the ranch whose origins and diet were exactly the same as the cimarrons'. Their multiple brands included a code for year of birth, which the *llaneros* knew but I did not; but my technique mystified them, since they did not know how to age horses from teeth.

## The Pottokas

Pottokas are native Basque ponies with Pleistocene origins. They seem to be the purest relics of a population of ponies that spread across the Pyrenees, the northern Spanish mountain ranges and into Portugal, during the last Ice Age. When the Celts arrived some 4,000 years ago from the east they brought with them their domesticated ponies, crossing them with this original race to produce the Portuguese *garrano*, the Galician pony, the Asturcón, Losino, Jaca Navarra and Merens. But the Celts had little influence on Basqueland, which has remained firmly Basque, and although a few pottokas show traces of the gentler Celtic blood introduced in the twentieth century, the great majority do not. Nor does their DNA show signs of domestication.

That a breed can escape the effects of domestication selection while living closely associated with people seems impossible, though reindeer have. Some pottokas have indeed been tamed and used, being bred from tame stock, but for the vast majority their only use is as cleaners of scrub on mountains and in woods. Pottokas, being a primitive breed, eat a far wider range of plants and shrubs than do domestic horses. Although colts are culled and stallions selected, the criteria for selection are not those used for domestic stallions. What is wanted is a stallion that can defend himself and look after his herd, not a candidate for producing pretty, tractable and adaptable children's ponies. Unconsciously, the Basques have preserved the original wild stock.

Wild pottokas are impossible to break with the traditional rather rough methods often used on Celtic ponies: they defend themselves as violently and desperately as they would against wolves or bears. Like deer or wild pigs, they can be completely tamed with patience, food and a great deal of understanding and skill. They are quite different from any other breed or type I have ever met, far more difficult to win over than previously untouched feral mustangs and cimarrons.

I wanted to set up a population of 'feral' horses for study purposes: for ethologists, equine students and horse-lovers in general to see at first hand how completely unmanaged horses choose to arrange their lives, and how different they are from domestic horses. Pottokas were the obvious choice. Starting with two natal bands, each with three mares pregnant by stallions other than the ones they were put with, the population has grown naturally since the project started in 2008. In 2016 there were four natal bands, which tend to break up rather in the winter and re-form in the spring, and a bachelor band. Their behaviour conforms exactly to that of feral horses elsewhere described in studies: they practise natal dispersal, have home ranges and stallion tiffs; they self-cure wounds and worm themselves by selecting medicinal plants.

They are not fed, handled or treated. They live on 1,200 hectares of mountain between 800 and 1,500m altitude in central Spain. The lower part is oak wood, with two deep gorges; the middle, mostly heather up to two metres high, with occasional patches of grass; the heights, grass, stones, Spanish broom, and heather. Thyme, espliego (a lavender-like plant), thistles, brambles, dog-rose, gorse, and willow and alder in the creeks are also common, and there are some fenced-off chestnut plantations. The ponies eat all the above-mentioned except alder. Autumn brings acorns[18], chestnuts and blackberries, so they fatten after the hot dry summers, when all but two springs can dry up.

There are two stallions and a filly that can be touched if you know how, but the rest cannot. However they are used to observers and ignore people sitting ten metres away. I do, of course, know all their ages and origins.

Most of our observations have been on social interactions, band structure and changes, band location according to weather and time of day, and especially leadership. I usually have at least one assistant, and some observations are made in groups during courses. Exact times of observation are difficult to give. We visit them some five hours a day, three times a week, at least four months a year and two or three times a week during the rest of the year; but they can be difficult to find.

## Other Populations Studied

### Mustangs in Pima County, Arizona

My first attempt to study wild horses instead of just watching them run away was both frustrating and enlightening. After a couple of days trudging about amid gnarled mesquite trees, sweet acacia and creosote bushes, listening to distant coyotes and finding lots of hoofprints, dung piles and rolling spots, I discovered an obviously popular green patch with a muddy waterhole, where I stayed a few days. They did come, but having to stay concealed in bushes limited my vision. However, patience paid off when a bachelor, after having laid siege to an old stallion for two days with the help of his bachelor buddies, moved in for the final battle, knocked the older horse off his feet and disappeared with the mares. Despite having watched other feral horses for a sum total of at least two years on end, it is the only time I have seen such a battle, and I did not see what happened after the old stallion struggled to his feet and set off in pursuit of the rustler. Studying rattlesnake ethology would have been more successful.

### Brumbies in the Snowy Mountains, Australia

Fourteen days of crawling about in snow while kookaburras hooted with laughter at my attempts to hide behind tiny bushes brought more success: in the wide, long valley with tree-lined slopes there were five good-sized natal bands and a bachelor band, never within sight of each other. At night they went up into the woods. They were fat, despite the winter, and fecund: most mares had a foal and a yearling in tow. But they were extremely wary, since people try to catch them. Here there were strong differences between the stallions. Alvaro was particularly alert to any disturbance, though there was no trace of other people. Bruce was so laid-back that his mares often wandered off grazing without his noticing; when he found himself alone he dashed about trying to sniff out their wandering trail. Cledwyn was especially fond of foals. Once, at nightfall when his large band was heading up to the woods, he noticed a mixed-sex group of five youngsters, two or three years old, that had been with Bruce the day before, on the valley floor. Cledwyn came down to investigate them, nuzzling the colts playfully, and then found himself in a quandary. Should he follow his fast-disappearing band, abandoning these little lost souls to the dingos, or should he protect them? He dithered up and down the slope, unable to decide, until one of them started to head upwards. That clinched the matter: he herded them vigorously up to join the band. But they were off on their own again the next day.[19]

### Baguales in Patagonia

On the edge of the Torres del Paine National Park, 120 feral horses live in a large herd together, never splitting up into bands. Their foals are heavily predated by puma. (More on these in Chapter 6.) I have observed them ten to fourteen days at a time, in 2013, 2014 and 2016.

### Cimarrons on Cotopaxi, Ecuador

The *páramo* of Cotopaxi is a vast, treeless apron spreading below the massive, rust-coloured snow-capped volcano. At 4,200m, the air is thin. After observing them for a week, I returned the next year with three other seasoned observers. In twelve intensive, twelve-hour days we catalogued 189 horses in twenty-three natal bands; nine had two stallions, an unusually high proportion. There were also three pairs without foals, two mixed-sex bands and twenty-five bachelors, usually in three bands graded by age. An unusual finding was that, out of seven skulls found, four were of four-year-old mares and two had deformities of the lower jaw and teeth (possibly due to inbreeding).

Used to seeing passing tourists, the horses admitted close observation (although a running Army recruit caused a mass stampede). Here the bands were often found grazing close together, or even intermingling, in select spots, so we concentrated our observations on inter-band interactions and the relations between stallions in two-stallion bands. Margrete Lie made an intensive study of soft mouth movements, finding them to occur after moments of tension, for instance after turning away from an encounter with a non-band member or, associated with yawning, when taking a break in the middle of a play bout.

## CHAPTER 4

# Natural Life, With Puma

## DISTURBING THE PEACE

Burnt-umber flatland sounds monotonous, and perhaps the monotony is precisely what makes the details spring out so vividly in the clear air: the tiny startling dots of scarlet ibis feeding several kilometres away; the *teru*, South America's lapwing, exploding from its unseen crouch to dive-bomb us away from its nest; the round eyes of the burrowing owls that pop up and down like jack-in-the-boxes; the unexpected crab shells underfoot, the bleached bones of a mare with a rotted jaw and a broken molar; a puma footprint.

I sit under a nut tree on the bank of the cordillera, for although the pink is only just fading from the dawn light and it is not yet hot, it soon will be. Out come the binoculars and notebook.

In front of me 150 horses speckle the plain. Some are in bands separated from all the others by a hundred metres or more, but other bands are closer together. Further away, a large group, comprising about half the horses, does not seem to be divisible into bands at all but looks like a homogenous mass. As usual, almost all the horses within view are eating; in the nearest bands I can often see a stallion standing to one side, gazing out over the savannah. Two foals are engaging in a singularly inefficient bout of mutual grooming: they have moved into appropriate positions but have not yet grasped why or what to do next. Other foals lie flat, invisible in the scruffy brown grass from which a bottle-brush tail flicks upwards for an instant from time to time. I start listing bands by identifying the stallions, chunkier and shinier than the rest, noting each band's position and its distance from others. Far off, at one end of the big block, I can see some swirling movements: the bachelor band, playing again. Those merry lads seem to live on air and giggles.

Suddenly a mare in a band nearby raises her head, swinging round rapidly to stare fixedly at a small clump of trees way over to the north, more than a kilometre away, her last mouthful of grass forgotten between her clamped jaws. Quickly the stallion comes to line up beside her and they stare side by side before he takes a couple of steps forward, head high, his muscles bulging with tension. His nose tips upwards for an instant as he sniffs the air. I drop the binoculars and start scrawling abbreviations. Already the other mares have caught the alarm and, glancing in the same direction at the sinister trees, are grouping together some lengths behind the stallion. The first mare, too, hurries back to them, calling her foal to her side as youngsters rush to join the rapidly forming assembly. They bunch together and stand waiting, staring at the stallion, or perhaps at what is beyond him in the deep, puzzling shadow of the trees.

Their hurried, purposeful grouping has caught the attention of a nearby band, which is similarly grouping together, catching the attention of a further one, so that a ripple of disturbance is passing over the plain like a breeze over a wheatfield. But there is no time to watch this: the stallion has whirled round to flee, the band doing the same so that as they all leap straight into a flat-out gallop he is last, following them. They head straight for the nearest band, which is already in full flight towards others, fusing together as they make for the main mass, itself already turning and starting to run. In a trice the speckles on the plain have consolidated into a solid mass of stampeding horses, raising dust as it goes.

This is an impressive sight no matter how many times you see it, a rocket-shaped cloud whose nether end is shrouded in swirling dust. Out front are the speedy youngsters, switching leads as they overtake each other, with the thickening stream following them. They must have covered a kilometre already and are showing no signs of slackening. Reaching scattered bushes, they sometimes all swerve in the same direction but sometimes the stream splits, only to unite again once past the bushes. If they keep going in a straight line they will have to split into many streams, for the bushes get thicker; but they do not. They all swing so they are heading at an angle towards the cordillera, and me. As they turn, I can see that what seemed from the side to be a solid mass of bodies is in fact full of holes: all the horses are galloping in their own space, with a gap of a metre or so between each horse and the next. Only the little foals are pressed to their mothers' sides.

As they fly towards me they wheel again to avoid crossing the cordillera and I can see quite clearly that the leaders are not the first to turn. The middle of the herd starts the turn and the leaders shift over to stay in front, so quickly that you can barely see it happening. As they stream past me I can see their outstretched necks, their hard-breathing nostrils, and the foals floating along effortlessly, their long legs matching their mothers' stride for stride. The ground trembles under their pounding hooves. Now they turn again, into the very centre of the savannah where there are no bushes; they are slowing down, especially the ones further back, dropping down to a trot as they disappear into a gully, raising clouds of dust. As the first ones reappear up the other side they are walking, spreading out so the close-packed stream that enters the gully disperses into diffuse eddies. But they do not stop: they keep walking, weaving in and out of each other's paths, circling, neighing – many sound like youngsters – to locate and re-form their bands. It will take time. Then, only then, will they rest.

It was a good one: nobody got left behind, no foals got stranded pitifully alone out there on the endless savannah, and it was not too long. They must have covered about four kilometres. Number 51 on my list, and I had a grandstand view. They have run in a huge open 'U', avoiding getting into the bushes on the east side and coming back, as so often, to the most open part of the savannah. There is an aftermath to come, so I cannot yet stop watching and covering the page with arrows and symbols; but when it is all really over I will re-write it all more neatly, since writing done without taking your eyes off the action looks distinctly drunken. Finally, after breakfast, it will all go into the tables. Annoyingly, I do not know exactly what started it off: something under trees.

*Horses are prey animals*. The central core of their being is immutably stamped with that evolutionary fact, which has fine-tuned their sense organs and reactions into being adapted to cope with the ever-present possibility of life-threatening danger. Studying the details of their defence tactics provides invaluable insights into these adaptations. We all know they run away from danger, but how, exactly?

## STUDYING PREDATOR DEFENCE BEHAVIOUR

There can be few better places to study predator defence behaviour than the *llanos*. The Camoruco cimarrons live with puma and jaguar, these predators in almost natural numbers since they are not hunted except when they kill calves right next to the ranch. The cimarrons live much further away and nobody cares if their foals get eaten. Puma are not big enough to take full-grown horses but they are a real threat to foals: we find two or three killed every year but most probably there are more since we do not make a metre-by-metre search of the whole area.

Living with predators makes the cimarrons particularly aware of real danger. In April, the time of our visits, the foals are small and at their most vulnerable. Anything that could be puma startles the horses instantly.

They share their enclosure with cattle that the *llaneros* regularly round up, basically by scaring and stampeding them in a controlled direction. The horses also stampede, reacting to mounted *vaqueros* as if they were another species of predator. Indeed, they react more instantly and far more nervously to the first appearance of mounted horsemen than do the cattle, which usually take some rousing before they start running. Between *llaneros* and possible puma, then, the horses perceive reasons to stampede about once a week or so, and perceive suspicious disturbances that make them prepare to flee, or at least move to a safer place, every day.

The clearness of the air, the lack of trees and the absolute flatness of the ground mean that with luck you can see the whole proceedings from start to finish. Sitting on the cordillera you have a grandstand view.

At first I could not see how to record the multiple, varied and simultaneous reactions of so many horses in any analysable form, but as patterns became clearer I developed a series of letters, symbols, and arrows that allows me, even years later, to reproduce the event in my mind's eye. Of course video recordings would help, but I would have to have the video camera running and pointing in the right direction at the right moment, a near-impossibility in practice. Most attempts show the horses already in full flight, not how the event started. Video also suffers the disadvantage of taking place within a frame, whereas in real life things well outside that frame can influence developments. Eyes and attention are remarkably flexible. They focus fast and the batteries do not run out. The best system is to have two observers, one watching and commenting while the other writes.

Not all responses to possible danger precipitate stampedes: some are false alarms that die down almost immediately, some doubts take longer to resolve, some provoke a band's less hasty removal to another place, and yet others are so instantaneous that their step-by-step evolution is compacted into a second (that's what frame-by-frame video analysis would elucidate). Reactions are graduated, although the elements that compose them are the same. As this became clearer I included non-escalating startles into the observations. Eliminating incomplete ones and those made prior to the development of the final notation, I ended up with ninety-eight complete, start-to-finish examples of predator defence behaviour.

## DEFENSIVE STEPS AND STRATEGIES

You can see most of the features I describe in domestic horses: predator defence behaviour is one of those deep-rooted innate patterns that do not change with domesticity. Briefly, the steps are:

1. Avoid places where danger lurks; conversely, stick to ones where safety is proven.
2. Live in bands in which one vigilant member can act as look-out for the rest when they are eating or sleeping.

3. As the first to spot any possible danger: react with alarm.
4. For others in the band: react immediately to this signal by bunching together ready for flight.
5. In flight, stay bunched, which means synchronizing speed and direction without colliding.
6. At the end of a real stampede, re-form the original bands, inevitably mixed up in flight.[20]

## 1. Avoidance

Puma use the cover of trees and bushes to approach prey. The cimarrons gave a wide berth to the wooded copses of Flor Amarillo, Flor Blanco and el Camoruco. Until 2011, when fevered horses entered them for shade during an epidemic of piroplasmosis, we had never found hoofprints or dung there. Apart from the puma danger there are vampire bats in the trees. The cattle, however, often rest there and the copses were strewn with their dung, footprints and bones.

The horses did not enter the woods at the north-east end of the enclosure, where jaguar lurk. Jaguar do not emerge onto open savannah; puma do, and hunt there. The horses' favourite grazing area was the very centre of the enclosure, where there are no bushes or cover. When they grazed among the acacia bushes to the east, they were more easily startled. Only very rarely did they visit the lush pasture of the drying lagoon in the north-east, surrounded by tall trees, and when they were there they fled at the slightest sound.

At the end of a stampede they always came to rest in the most open, safest part of the savannah. For the first few days of the first course, they ran away on spotting us from afar. We arrived from the west at first light, when there is always an easterly breeze, so we were downwind from them. Each time they ran a huge semi-circle to end up in this safest part of the savannah downwind from us before stopping to stare. We could see them raise their heads to sniff the breeze, a lovely sight. Later they became used to us and did not run away.

At nightfall they crossed the little ridge, the cordillera, to spend the night in the extreme south, where there are cattle pens along the fence. Here, the grazing is poor but there is no cover at all. At first light, before dawn, they crossed back over the cordillera northwards to reach better grazing. They either had to pass between the copses or make a long detour eastwards to emerge into the acacia bushes. Crossing between the copses tended to make them nervous. They could not see the other side and stopped often; sometimes they made a run for it, and sometimes crossed in bunches. Other days they were perfectly calm and went quietly in strings. We did not know what made the difference, except that when we camped in Flor Amarillo they did not cross there but used the longer route, although they moved at around five o'clock when no one was yet out of a hammock. What happened in the night may have dictated how, where and when they crossed. In 2011 they always waited longer before crossing at six o'clock or so. That year we found puma tracks with cubs several times on the trail to Flor Amarillo, and the young mare Gitanilla (little gypsy) lost what appeared to be a perfectly healthy foal, her first, within a day of birth.

The cimarrons' patterns of avoidance may be called cultural, in the sense that there are places that they never go to without individuals learning why not from first-hand experience.

In populations with home ranges, like the pottokas, horses have an intimate knowledge of every path, inclination and stone, so they can run away even in poor visibility and know which are safe places to make for. Uphill is the most usual choice.

Domestic horses, too, are reluctant to re-approach places they associate with alarm or fear.

## 2. Living in Bands

Except in unusual circumstances, feral horses are not found alone. They live in bands. Eating, which takes up 60–80 per cent of their time, is a noisy affair that precludes predator detection, as does the low head position. Sleeping is wholly incompatible with vigilance. Only in a band can a horse eat or sleep in relative safety while another band member maintains the look-out for all. Mares stand over their small foals while these sleep, as do some stallions.

## Vigilance

Usually in a grazing or resting band, one member is on watch, especially in early morning and late afternoon, predators' favourite hunting hours; at midday, vigilance may be relaxed. According to our figures stallions are twice more likely to be vigilant than mares; they also raise their heads twice as often to look around during grazing.[21] Stallions do not have such high nutritional requirements as mares, who have to spend most of their time eating; but stallions have to eat too, and when they do a mare watches. A stallion's most usual position is on the outskirts of a band or behind it, so his view of the exterior world is not cluttered by other bodies, although he can see all his band.

A horse's head position indicates his level of arousal (see Fig. 4.3). Asleep on his feet, a horse lets the nuchal ligament support the weight of his head, which hangs with the tips of the ears just below the withers. Resting but not asleep, the forehead is level with the withers. A vigilant horse's head is slightly higher, with the cheekbones, halfway between the eyes and nostrils, level with the withers, and the ears pointing in the direction of the binocular part of the visual field as he scans the savannah for movement.[22]

Vigilance in itself would not be helpful without other band members' capacity to perceive and react to signs that the lookout has spotted a possible threat. Stability and peace in a band help optimize both vigilance and communication.

## 3. Alarm

On spotting a possible threat, the horse swings round to face it if necessary (orientation) and raises his head suddenly, bringing the muzzle level with the withers (alarm posture). The

*Fig. 4.1    Bambú turns to watch us, vigilant but not alarmed, as his mares pass by.*

Fig. 4.2    *Vigilance: a pottoka mare stands guard over her foal, with about half her head above the level of the withers.*

Fig. 4.3    *The level of the horse's head in relation to the withers reveals his state of arousal.* Left: *when a horse is asleep on his feet, his head hangs low, supported by the nuchal ligament.* Left centre: *drowsy but not fully asleep, with the ears about level with the withers.* Right centre: *in vigilance, the middle of the head is level with the withers.* Right: *in alarm, the muzzle is level with or above the withers. (Drawing: Carmen Manzana Mañero)*

sudden raising of the head causes tension in the back muscles, raising the tail. The brusque-ness of the action, which is always abrupt, catches the eye of other members of the band. Ears are pointed at the disturbance; the binocular part of the visual field is directed at it, and the horse may flare his nostrils as he sniffs the air, an action facilitated by raising the muzzle to a more horizontal position, albeit briefly.

In fact alarm causes tension to rise in all muscle groups; though as some are naturally stronger than others, particular bodily effects are produced. The jaws are clenched firmly shut by the great masseter muscle, while the splenius in the upper neck raises the head. Tension in the back and articular muscles causes short, jerky steps.[23]

The alarm position is shown even by isolated horses, so it is not a social signal like head-thrusting (threat). However, other horses react to it by becoming alarmed themselves.

### Causes of alarm

While any movement, sound, vibration, or smell (which we, with our poor sense of smell, may not detect) may cause alarm, not all do, partly because of individual habituation, partly

Fig. 4.4    Humo in alarm posture. So far, only four mares have noticed, but are vigilant rather than alarmed.

Fig. 4.5    The stallion Guapo in alarm posture, with his muzzle at the level of the withers. The mares glance at the 'danger' and hurry to bunch behind him.

because of social learning and partly because of herd culture. Small foals are alarmed even by butterflies, but soon habituate to them, taking their cue from their mothers' nonchalant attitude. Colts, who spend increasing amounts of time with their fathers, seem to become more sensitized to some cues than to others, perhaps as a result of learning from their fathers' reactions. As a matter of culture, the cimarrons run away at the sight of mounted *llaneros* but not from us on foot; other populations do not necessarily do the same. In fact the cimarrons do not need to flee from *llaneros*, who do not want to muster them; they do so because they always have done.

Sources of primary alarm are: movement that might be puma, especially fast, unidentified movement; any sign of movement in bushes; brusque or rapid movement even from identified sources (like students turning a page too rapidly or swatting mosquitoes); mounted *llaneros*; sounds in bushes; shouts from invisible *llaneros*. Sources of secondary, or transmitted, alarm are: another horse in alarm posture or alarmed movement; the sight of bunching and/or fleeing in distant bands; the sound or vibration of invisible horses galloping.

While alarming sights usually provoke staring and attempts at identification before flight, alarming sounds often set bands into instant flight without orientation or any attempt to identify the source. Once a yearling went to visit the bachelors and, taking a shortcut back to his band, floundered about in scrubby undergrowth, provoking the whole herd into an instant stampede. The bachelors, who had watched his progress, stood unmoved, gazing at the mass panic with interest.

Horses' superhuman ability to perceive and analyse movement extends to perceiving its purpose or pattern. *Llaneros* ride at a jog-trot whether they are moving through or setting up to herd; although both circumstances look the same initially the horses ignore the former and flee at the latter, even when we cannot tell what the *llaneros* are up to until later. Similarly, if we move slowly and steadily towards them they run away; if we wander about like a group of aimless animals, we arrive much closer without alarming them.

## 4. Communication of Alarm

Any horse, even a foal, can show orientation and alarm, provoking the same in others. However, since the stallion is the most likely to be the most vigilant, the majority of band alerts are started by him. When another has snapped suddenly into the alarm posture, the stallion rapidly comes to stand next to him, sharing the alarmed horse's direction of gaze. He then usually takes a few steps forward, making himself the nearest of the band to the threat while he evaluates it. If he is on the other side of the band but is the first to notice the threat, he runs through the band to take up this position between the others and the threat.

At the sight of their stallion alarmed the mares raise their heads, show alarm and, with backward glances in the direction of the threat, move to bunch some five metres behind the stallion. Their movements are purposeful and hurried, alerting others and provoking them to do the same. Noticeably, a horse who has apparently not seen or not reacted to the stallion's snapping into alarm joins in with this bunching on seeing others deliberately drawing together, just as the sight of people rushing to investigate an accident provokes others innocent of the cause to do the same. They remain in a bunch, though separated by a metre or so from each other, watching the stallion.

This is the sequence of a typical alarm; but there are many variations. If there are other males above the age of three or so in the band, they come to stand parallel with the stallion, usually a little more than a metre away. Often one inserts himself between two others, so they

*Fig. 4.6   Mares on Cotopaxi bunched behind their stallion. Both he and the farthest youngster are in alarm posture, but the mares are vigilant rather than alarmed. (Photo: Javier Solis)*

move aside to maintain this distance from each other. If there are no males, a mare may do the same, but only if the stallion has been staring in the same direction in alarm for more than a couple of minutes without fleeing.

The stallion may advance a couple of steps before stopping, all the time in alarm; he may snort loudly. If he makes no further move except to stand staring, the mares, after several minutes, relax and gradually resume other activities.

## 5. Flight

Horses avoid anything they find threatening, but how fast and far they go varies. Initially the stallion's assessment and reaction cues the behaviour of the rest of the band. Rifa saw the same in Asturcón ponies.

Despite the hugely variable response to the variable threats, three factors are always noticeable: bunching; synchrony of movement, gait and direction; and collision avoidance.

### Bunching, or cohesion

Horses' primary reaction to alarm is to bunch together, producing the predator's eye confusion effect (Pulliam 1973) a common defence strategy among social prey animals. Predators have different killing or immobilizing tactics, often involving attack at different, select points of the

*Fig. 4.7    Running away together in a close-packed formation confuses the predator's eye so that he cannot distinguish where to attack.*

body. Faced with scores of bodies streaming past, merging together, the predators cannot distinguish their mark. For a prey animal without refuge like a horse, isolation is dangerous.

If there is time, bunching precedes flight. Some stampedes start so instantaneously that the horses are already galloping before they have time to bunch, so they close ranks as they go. But when the stallion has snapped into the alarm posture without moving, the mares bunch behind him, watching him. The alarm in their movements prompts the youngsters to move towards them.

Similarly, the reaction of an outlying horse on being startled is to rush into the middle of the nearest band, while a startled foal heads instantly for his mother.

Once in flight, a band hurtles towards the nearest visible band and so on until the whole herd is stampeding.

Hamilton, in a seminal paper entitled 'Geometry for the selfish herd', proposed that prey animals live in groups for entirely selfish reasons: the middle of the herd is the safest place to be when an attack comes. While single frightened animals do seek the centre of a calm band, I do not see horses jostling to be in the centre of a band or herd during flight. Rather, the point seems to be fusion, loss of identity. The single horse loses individual identity in the band; the band loses its identity in bigger groupings, which fuse into a herd; finally, if the cattle are running too, the herd fuses with their herd and loses its identity among them (they do not seem to realize that, being all shades of colour instead of white like the cattle, they are still very visible).

I call bunching, or cohesion, a primary ploy not only because it precedes fleeing, but because it can override moving directly away from a source of danger. If an individual or band has to choose between running directly away from danger but alone, or running to pass the danger to reach others, the horse (or band) chooses the latter. We saw this most frequently when the truck came too fast to pick us up, bouncing and rattling, and its trajectory cut between one or two bands and the main mass. The bands ran across its path to reach the others, rather than away from it. I have seen the same phenomenon several times when sounds in the copses startled bands nearby, and more distant bands ran towards and then past the source to join them. When an Army runner startled many bands on Cotopaxi, the bands furthest from him ran diagonally towards him to join a mass of fleeing horses. Losing one's identity in the mass is safer than running away alone.[24]

## Synchrony

Doing what others are doing, moving together and turning together, is what keeps the herd united in flight from start to finish.

At first, the rest of the band synchronizes with the stallion, so let us go back to him. We have left him standing staring, with the rest of the band bunched behind. What happens next depends on his judgement of the seriousness of the danger.

If he is more perplexed than frightened, he may take a few steps forward, still in alarm posture. He may snort loudly. He may take a few steps to one side, then the other, getting a lateral view with one eye and then the other. If sons, bachelors or other males have lined up beside him, they all behave like a synchronized team, matching steps and attitudes as they weave to and fro like a line of chorus girls. Any horse who makes a change provokes the same change in all the others.

If the stallion rates the disturbance as minimal but disagreeable, he turns and walks away. Simultaneously the watching band behind him does so too, so he is now walking behind them. If they start to trot, so does he. If he stops, turning to assess the threat again, they usually do not, but keep walking, so he turns back to follow them again. That is, he is now synchronizing with them. But if he hurries to catch up with them they usually start trotting too.

If he rates the threat as medium-grade, he turns and trots away, after the band since they have already synchronized with his actions.

If the threat is serious, he whirls round and gallops, after them since they are already doing the same. The stallion Jotero often overtook his band, but most stallions, on reaching it, do not. The band heads for other bands that, noticing the alarm, are usually already bunched and in flight, even when the source of the alarm was invisible to them: that is, both individuals and whole bands react to the sight of bunching and fleeing by doing the same themselves. A stampede of the whole herd may follow, weaving its way over the savannah swerving unanimously to right or left to avoid bushes, or splitting round them only to bunch together again the other side. Keeping together and doing the same thing together is the main ploy.

In a stampede the front runners are youngsters, the fastest of the herd, who swap leads continually. But they are not leading the herd: they too are synchronizing with the majority that they can see behind them. This is particularly clear in cattle round-ups. The *llaneros* drive the mixed herd straight towards the cordillera, which they will pass over to reach the pens beyond. The experienced horses who, being older and slower, are in the centre and rear of the herd, know that if they swerve off to the right before reaching the cordillera they will be left alone, for the *llaneros* only want the cattle. As the mixed herd thunders towards the cordillera, you can see the centre and rear horses change direction a fraction of a second before the front ones, who then shift to the right and turn too. Synchrony is not a case of blindly following leaders but of doing what the majority are doing, whether they are in front or behind.

In flight, horses also synchronize gait and speed. When all are galloping flat-out this is not obvious, for inevitably some gallop slower than others, who do not wait for them. However, in less urgent flights, when trotting or walking away will suffice, the whole band goes at the same speed. The same is seen at the end of a flight after the immediate danger is over, when the slower members of the herd drop to trot and then walk before the younger, more energetic front runners do so, and thus influence the latter to slow down too.

Foals who cannot keep up in flight but find themselves left behind simply stop running. There is no other body with which to synchronize. Sick or lame horses, though, keep trudging after the herd as best they can or, as we have sometimes seen, seek refuge amongst the cattle if these are quiet.

Fig. 4.8   As the baguales in Torres del Paine, Patagonia, begin to flee they bunch together, presenting what looks like a solid mass of bodies.

Fig. 4.9   When they turn away from us, the spaces between them become clear.

### Collision avoidance

Colliding and falling in flight means death if a predator is behind. Collision is avoided by maintaining a space between bodies of a little more than a metre's distance. When the whole herd wheels these spaces are clearly seen and evenly marked. The only individuals who do not maintain space are the foals, who run close beside their mothers.

Collision avoidance, or respect for individual space, is taught especially by mature mares to youngsters in the course of everyday life, through aggression. Although the proximal causes of aggression are varied (*see* Chapter 6), the message is always the same: *get out of my space*. The final cause is to avoid collision in flight. Significantly, in both the case of a horse moving away from an aggressor and that of a stampede, fear is involved.

Collisions with bushes and clumps of undergrowth are, of course, also avoided. If the herd is dashing straight towards an obstacle, it may split into two as one horse goes right and his neighbour left, both shifting their neighbours across to right or left as space is maintained. After the obstacle the herd comes together again, like a stream flowing round a rock.

## 6. Re-Forming Bands

A real stampede can last for half an hour and cover several kilometres; lesser flights die down more quickly. The horses always head for the most open part of the savannah; they may even gallop round in a circle there before slowing. As panic dies down, so does speed until the herd trots, then walks.

Reaching a walk, the horses spread out somewhat, though they keep moving in the same direction together: that is, the cohere imperative loses its importance once safety is reached, though synchrony is maintained for longer. They then begin to look for foals, yearlings and fellow band members, neighing and weaving in and out of each other's paths. Finally, coordinated herd movement stops, giving way to the search for band identity.

Some ten to twenty minutes after the end of a real stampede, when all the bands have located their members, they form what we call *piñas*, a term coined by Vanesa Ugarte.

*Piña* is the Spanish for pinecone or pineapple, but it is also used to denote a huddle of people conferring together, as do American rules footballers deciding their next tactics. When bands form *piñas* all the members except the stallion stand in a semi-circle or 'U', with their heads facing inwards. Their shoulders are often fairly crowded together, as when resting together. The stallion stands across the open side of the semi-circle or 'U', placed so that the breeze passes over his body into the centre space left by the horses' heads: that is, they breathe and are bathed in his smell. They remain like that for at least fifteen minutes and up to half an hour before moving.

When bands form *piñas* they are separated from each other by at least thirty metres. They exclude non-members of the band aggressively, so that there are always a few floating youngsters left out of any *piña*. Since the breeze comes from the same direction for all, the effect of six or eight bands in *piña* is striking, since all are oriented in the same direction, dotted across the savannah.

Some bands do not form a distinct *piña*, and we have seen *piñas* only after a major stampede. After lesser flights, bands do group together as they do when resting, but they do not necessarily adopt this strictly oriented formation or stand so close together.

The *piña* has not been described in any other study, so I do not know whether it is a particular feature of this population or whether other researchers have not been so fortunate in seeing the end of so many stampedes. It is a definite formation, unlike the higgledy-piggledy arrangements seen in resting bands, which do not exclude non-members.

The orientation of the stallion to the breeze suggests that the *piña* reaffirms band unity with him, which has temporarily been obliterated in the confusion and terror of the stampede. The members of the band literally breathe their stallion, but do not allow outsiders to do so. The fact that bands do not form true *piñas* at other times, or after minor flights when band unity has not been lost, supports this idea.

## SELF-ORGANIZING COLLECTIVE MOVEMENT

At first I did not realize the significance of the three flight factors, cohesion, synchrony and collision avoidance, or even identify them clearly as such, although I saw them in action again and again. What I was seeing seemed so infinitely fluid and variable that even description baffled me, let alone analysis. I was sure that somebody must have looked at this phenomenon of mass movement, because it is so common in nature. Little trout zigzagging together, or a flock of pigeons wheeling together in the sunlight so that all their wings are bright white one second and disappearing dark the next; sheep trickling down a mountainside to become streams, rivers and finally a flood of bodies; deer bounding together up a hillside, or a whirling swarm of bees circling dizzily yet making its way across the fields; meerkats like synchronized swimmers; a herd of cimarrons in full flight, weaving their way across the plain: these are sights that lift our hearts with their beauty, filling us with wonder. Surely someone had worked on the mystery of how they do it.

I say 'they', because we humans are no good at it. Human stampedes usually result in someone being trampled to death as people crash into each other. Moving in synchrony is not our talent. Army recruits need weeks of practice, shouted orders and rigid ranks and files before they can wheel like pigeons. Chorus girls and synchronized swimmers work hard to achieve what meerkats do naturally. Even three-legged races tax us.

Perhaps that is why we marvel at the spectacle; perhaps too, that is why ethologists did not seem to have applied themselves to the phenomenon. At any rate my Internet searches drew blanks. I was using the wrong words.

The eureka moment came when I was sitting on a sofa with a friend's children watching *The Lion King*. When the wildebeest stampeded down the gulch, hundreds of bodies streaming together, separating round rocks and coming together again in a truly lifelike sequence, I was transfixed. *How had they done that?* It had to be the key. My new searches led me to Craig Reynolds, whose work made that sequence possible.

Craig Reynolds is a computer animator with a passion for lifelike behavioural animation. Instead of looking at the overall behaviour of a flock of birds, he reasoned that every member of it is an autonomous character that determines its own actions. In massed flight, it is conscious of itself, its immediate neighbours and maybe a few surrounding characters, but not of a distant and perhaps invisible leader. Scattering little triangles to represent birds ('boids', he calls them) at random on a computer screen, he gave each one just three instructions to guide its movements: cohere or move towards others, match direction and velocity with them (what I am calling synchrony), and do not collide. On pressing START, they gradually came together into a unified flock, flowing around the screen in a lifelike way. This is self-organizing behaviour. Instead of following a predetermined order, coordinated mass movement emerges from the rules that individuals follow to determine their movements. It needs no fixed leaders or directors if all follow the same guidelines, a behavioural algorithm that applies whether there are five or five hundred individuals in the group. When the group nears an obstacle, the one about to collide with it turns, so the others beside it do too, and there is now a different 'boid' in front as the group sets off in another direction. By changing the relative values of the three components, looser or more unified movement is produced.

Reynolds published his algorithmic solution to the mystery in *Computer Graphics*, not the first journal ethologists reach for, so its ethological importance took time to have an impact. But it has led to a rapidly expanding new field of ethology: the study of emergent or self-organizing behaviour in flocks, shoals and swarms (Couzin and Kreuse 2003, Conradt and Roper 2003, Sumpter 2006). Its influence is spreading as more and more instances of its application are found in the type of movements given above: flocks of pigeons, teams of meerkats, swarms of bees, shoaling fish.

*Fig. 4.10    The formula bunch–synchronize–avoid collision is the basis of herding, when the herder startles animals into flight and controls their direction through their reluctance to collide with him.*

Increasingly, mass movements and especially mass flight in prey animals are found to be self-organizing, as a moment's thought shows they must be. In the flurry and terror provoked by attack, a pre-ordained leader or director might be invisible, absent or already dead. Changes of direction, especially reversals, bring new animals to the fore, a position that any must be able to take. What is also necessary is that the animals have lateral perception, to know what their neighbours are doing. Fish have lateral lines, and manage to cohere, synchronize and avoid collisions in three dimensions. Horses have lateral eyes.

Sheep, while grazing, show relaxed adherence to the three-part algorithm, but as soon as they start to move, its influence becomes more binding. The faster they move, the more firmly it applies (Gautrais *et al.* 2007, Michelina *et al.* 2008). Fish and birds do the same in three dimensions (Axelsen *et al.* 2001). More and more examples of synchrony, doing what the others are doing, are found, from vigilant behaviour in kangaroos to the mass escape of baboons leaping through trees.

### Who initiates changes?

Of course, somebody has to start the whole thing off. Does it matter who does so? In the slow-starting flights I saw in horses, it was almost always the stallion, but some were started by a frightened outlying horse dashing into the centre of a band. On the other hand, the horse might be calmed by the imperturbable calm of the band, and fall to doing what they were doing: grazing, usually. Frightened foals do not provoke flight, but yearlings can. Is there some pattern as to who initiates changes?

Once Vanesa and I were trying to shelter under a pathetic bush when the whole herd walked straight towards us, disturbed by *llaneros*. Surprised by these crouched figures with black cubes for faces, they turned right and started trotting, then galloping, streaming past us. But as soon as they passed us, they turned and came back, passing us again. They reminded me of a shoal of little trout zigzagging together in shallows. To and fro they went, sometimes speeding up, sometimes swinging their heads to stare at us, sometimes slowing or even stopping before setting off again. They wanted to identify us, but nervousness overtook them. Finally they just stopped and stared.

I have seven minutes of video of this remarkable display, with one break in it about halfway through. Although, at normal speed, the herd appears to be in perfect synchrony in any

Fig. 4.11    Head-turning as the cimarrons pass us, initiated by Jotero (left, grey), followed by Bambú (black) and spreading to others behind Jotero.

change, frame-by-frame analysis shows one horse initiating the change a split second before others react. There are sixty-one changes of various types: changes of cohesion; changes of gait, upwards or downwards; stops; changes of direction, veering or reversing completely; swinging the head to look at us; changes of leader. As there were 146 horses, not counting foals, when I get them all in I cannot see who initiates a change; when there are only about thirty I can. That leaves forty-seven changes where I can identify the initiator and who synchronizes with the change but, maddeningly, I cannot always tell whether it spreads to the whole herd, although the direction reversals always do. Since they all have short tails I sometimes cannot be certain which are juvenile. Here's a summary of the results:

1. The faster they go (gait) the more they cohere, losing band identity. Conversely, as they drop to a walk, they separate into clumps that are bands, with a few stragglers in between.
2. When cohesion and speed are high, the whole herd synchronizes. When both are low, synchrony within bands is maintained, but that between bands may be lost.
3. Leaders change continually and may be any age or sex. At one point a two-year-old leads after passing his mother, continuing in the lead although she gradually drops back, overtaken by others. He (or she) provokes two direction shifts (veers) of the whole herd before being overtaken.
4. Changes of any type can spread to horses in front of, as well as behind or beside, the initiator.
5. Initiators of gait changes may be any age or sex. Once, a foal breaks into canter to keep up with his mother, starts all those behind cantering and, as these overtake the trotters ahead, they start cantering too until the whole herd is cantering. Other upward transitions are started as the herd passes us and one accelerates nervously.
6. Being directly alongside another, or passing another, induces gait synchrony. For instance a trotting horse passing a walking one may start walking, or may induce the other to trot.
7. Turning the head to look at us, without changing gait or direction, was most often initiated by males (6/10, with two mares and two unknowns). The initiator was never in the lead but was in the foreground, that is, closest to us. Twice, the nearest horses did not follow suit, but those further in front and behind did.
8. Turning the head followed by complete reversal of direction (whole herd) was most often initiated by males (6/7, five being bachelors and the other a stallion; one unknown). They were never in the lead. On the four occasions when I can identify the actors, the initiator of the head-turn was not the horse who changed direction first.
9. Turning the head and stopping, staring at us, was most often initiated by males (6/9 definitely male, five being bachelors; others unknown), never in the lead but closest to us.
10. As the performance continued, the horses in the foreground became more predominantly male, with the mares hidden behind them. All the bachelors were in the foreground.

There are also four sequences of detailed movement synchrony. Three involve stallion-bachelor pairs (Jotero/Bambino, Jotero/Chocolate, Humo/Chocolate). I do not know paternal relationships but obviously not all are father/son pairs, nor were the bachelors living in the stallions' bands. In all three cases, the pair weaves from side to side, examining us with one eye and then the other, moving their legs and heads in unison like mirror images, a few steps one way, a few steps the other, a perfect *pas de deux*. The stallion starts the action but when the bachelor becomes too alarmed and starts to trot away, the stallion does too.

The fourth example makes people laugh. Two bachelors stand side by side facing us. The one on the right swings his head left rapidly to dislodge a fly on his flank. Almost simultaneously the one on the left turns his head left rapidly too, only to wonder why: there is nothing interesting to look at.

This frame-by-frame analysis shows, firstly, a prime example of Reynolds' three-part algorithm (I will call it the flight algorithm) in action. Secondly, it shows that any horse can initiate a change, even though investigative changes are more likely to be initiated by males than others. But if all are doing the same thing, how are there any changes? The question introduces the third point: that a horse who initiates a change is one with particular motivation to do so. From then on, the synchrony factor takes over: that is, unless he has a particular motivation to do otherwise, a horse will do what others are doing.

Three kinds of change illustrate this. Turning the head to look at us, whether in passing or as a preliminary to direction reversal or stops, was predominantly initiated by males, particularly bachelors. Of all age and sex classes, bachelors are the most inquisitive. Their future role as stallions will be to identify risks, and they spend their formative years identifying and evaluating them. The most agile, fastest and, biologically speaking, the most expendable of the herd, they are the boldest and most motivated to investigate the unknown.

Fig. 4.12    Seven bachelors of the bagual herd investigate us in synchrony. The eighth, to the right, lags behind.

Fig. 4.13    In a typical all-male parallel line-up, the eighth bachelor runs to insert himself between the fourth and fifth of the previous photo.

One upward change to canter was initiated by a foal motivated to keep up with his trotting mother. One whole-herd slow-down was initiated by a scrawny mare who dropped to a walk, apparently tired.

Motivation, that tricky subject, provokes change from the mainstream activity. Having no particular motivation, horses synchronize with the rest. Most clearly, fear enhances both synchrony and cohesion. I see fear sweep through the herd like a wave, a kind of emotional synchrony.

Those who work on self-organizing behaviour do not mention fear or emotional synchrony, for the good reason that it smacks of anthropomorphism, thinking we know what an animal is feeling. On what do I base my opinion that they are more or less frightened?

Experience in observation is my only guide. I look at head position, mouth tension, quality of movement, speed and what amounts to general impression. I deal with frightened horses almost daily, and risk my life on my judgement; I teach people to recognize fear and they find my teaching reliable. But, infuriatingly, there are no studies that relate what we see to objective physiological measures.[25] We only have experience, usually painfully won, to guide us.

The sheep study showed that cohesion and synchrony increase with speed, which, in sheep, increases with fear. I would say the primary variable is fear rather than speed. In the most dramatic examples of synchrony and cohesion in the video as in other observations, when the stallion-bachelor pairs moved like mirror images, they were not going at speed but at a tense, cautious walk. They were investigating.

## SUMMARY OF DEFENCE REACTIONS

To sum up: defence tactics in the face of predator attack take the form of massed flight, a self-organizing behaviour in which each individual's actions are guided by the flight algorithm, producing coordinated, synchronized group action.

- Cohesion is the primary response to alarm.
- Stallions usually initiate flight, in which synchrony is marked. Cohesion within bands precedes cohesion between bands, which fuse into a homogeneous herd in flight.
- Collisions are avoided by not entering the individual space of neighbours.
- Changes during flight can be initiated by any particularly motivated member and spread almost instantaneously through the herd.
- Fear enhances adhesion to the flight algorithm, in investigation as well as flight.
- A band's distancing itself from threat is not an all-or-nothing response but is graduated according to perception of the seriousness of the threat according to individual habituation, social learning and culture.

*    *    *    *

The graduated adherence to the flight algorithm provokes the question: if it is, so to speak, like the operation of a dimmer switch, producing stronger or weaker effects according to the extent that all share the same motivation, when does it get switched off entirely? Or is it always on, although dimly, even in calm moments?

To answer these questions, we must reconsider how horses go about their daily lives in the light of the flight algorithm and its implications.

## CHAPTER 5

# Social Life Revisted

The social lives of horses reflect their adaptation to their ecological niche as grazing prey animals. The factors of the flight algorithm describe their social system, that of self-organizing bands whose autonomous members have different roles or motivation according to age and sex. These factors are present in all their social activities. Since horses live in company all the time, all their activities are social. They are always aware of others around them: their placing, their attitudes, their activities and their state of arousal.

## COHESION AND SYNCHRONY

First, bands are cohesive. A band is a band because its members stay together. They are not scattered randomly across vast tracts of land. A member who has inadvertently lost sight of others neighs to relocate them, and comes back to the band. Cohesion starts at birth, when foals move towards and follow their mothers. We can call this strong innate urge cohesion or gregariousness, or say they are social animals or seek company: these are different ways of expressing the same innate psychological necessity. Social isolation is one of the greatest contributors to behavioural stress in domestic horses, notably expressed in stereotypical behaviour. They want to be together, to cohere.

Secondly, the members of a band synchronize their activities. Their main ones are eating, resting and marching from one place to another. They do these all together, so synchrony keeps the band unified. Rifa saw that bands of Asturcón ponies were 80 per cent synchronized when eating and resting; on the march, they were 100 per cent synchronized.

A study on ibex groups examined the reasons for incomplete synchrony in maintenance activities, and found again that motivation was a determinant. Different maintenance require-

Fig. 5.1   *Band synchrony in grazing, Los Camarucos. Note that the distance between the mare and her yearling is smaller than that between the adults.*

Fig. 5.2   Synchrony in investigation, pottoka bachelors.

ments give animals different motivation. For instance, lactating mothers have higher food requirements than youngsters, while youngsters need to play, learn to interact socially, and learn about their surroundings. In a grazing group, then, all may be eating together, but at other times the mothers will be eating while the youngsters are playing, learning or resting. In ibex these differences finally lead to the formation of different sub-groups that split apart entirely and synchronize within themselves (Ruckstuhl and Neuhaus 2001). In horses the same occurs. A grazing band is often composed of a central core of nursing mothers busily eating, flanked by a group of youngsters doing their own thing. Colts, whose necessities are quite different from mares', go off into a bachelor band whose members share their motivation. But when all have the same motivation, as when all are frightened, synchrony is complete. During investigation, where there is also an element of fear, youngsters often show that mirror-image synchrony seen in my video.

Directional synchrony also occurs during grazing. On Cotopaxi I watched bands grazing and noted their body directions every five minutes. Over 70% of the time their bodies were aligned within the same 30° of arc, regardless of wind direction or slope. When one turned, slowly the rest did too, so that in some of my direction diagrams all the horses are facing the same way, but in others one horse is in the middle of turning, sometimes with another following his turn. In essence, this is the same band movement as the herd direction changes in the Venezuela video, but in slow motion and on a smaller scale. Since the horses are not frightened, the spaces between them are bigger and they do not have to be so exactly lined up to avoid colliding. Horses do swing from side to side as they graze (covering about 30° of arc), since they eat round one forefoot, then advance the other and eat round that one.[26]

*Fig. 5.3   Band synchrony, Cotopaxi. In the foreground, the stallion Brillante keeps watch while NegB (far left) and the mares rest. Behind, maxi-bachelors graze. The fourth from the left, attracted by the mares, has turned, provoking his neighbour to turn too. Half a minute later all had turned, maintaining synchrony. (Photo: Javier Solis)*

*Fig. 5.4   The bagual herd shows directional synchrony or alignment while ending a feeding bout and beginning to rest.*

A similar series of observations on the pottokas shows the same thing.

During marches the whole band moves in a string, with the stallion behind. If the front horse stops, they all stop; if s/he changes direction, they all do.

Band marches do not have fixed leaders. In 2010 a student, Nicolás de la Hermosa (after whom the Nicos were named) collected 211 observations of cimarron marches and could not see any fixed leader except in very small bands. When there was only one mare with a youngster and a stallion, the mare did initiate marches, but if there were several mares any one could initiate the march. As they went along, youngsters often ran out in front. Our observations on pottoka bands showed the same, as did those of Bourjade and others in Przewalski's horses. Kreuger and others (2013) confirmed the same in feral horses.

The α leader mare is a myth. No single character initiates or leads marches or changes of activity.

What provokes others to follow is determined, purposeful leaving. When that does not work the horse comes back and leaves again in the same way until they do. If they have a particular reason not to, they won't. I saw a beautiful example of this in the brumbies in the Snowy Mountains. They liked to lick salt off the road at its lowest point crossing the valley, but only after dark, when they could see car headlights approaching from the ridge and scurry into hiding. A young mare wanted to go before nightfall, and tried again and again to get the others to follow, but only at dusk would they do so.

The initiator of a march is the one most highly motivated to start marching. Feral horse marches often lead to water. A lactating mare, whose water requirements are high, gets thirsty first and usually starts these marches. Obviously her foal will follow, her yearling too, and maybe her two-year-old, so already a sizeable part of the band is moving and influencing the rest to move too. Often youngsters start scampering ahead, but if they have chosen the wrong route they realign themselves in front, as dogs do when out walking with us.

What started the α mare leader myth? Perhaps it was Tyler's observation that her New Forest pony bands did often have clear leaders. But hers was not a natural population. There were few stallions, and most bands were composed of one or two mares, their foals and female offspring (colts are culled). One mare may be bolder or more experienced than the other, so the other habitually follows her, as do the youngsters. In the larger feral bands this is not the case.

Another student, Victor Ros, suggested that there are three types of band movement: marches towards, marches away from, and drifts. Marches towards lead to water, to new grazing, to a breezy spot in summer, or to no apparent end point except that when they get there, they stop suddenly. In the pottokas any horse can start these, but lactating mares start

*Fig. 5.5   Band march led by lactating mare, Cotopaxi. The stallion follows. (Photo: Javier Solis)*

*Fig. 5.6    Similar band march led by foal and youngster. (Photo: Javier Solis)*

water marches. The stallion almost invariably follows the rest passively, without any signs of directing them.

Away-from marches start from some disturbance. They are not flights but mass avoidance that starts a march longer than is necessary for simple avoidance: for the pottokas, rowdy tourists, hunters or motorbikes. One old pottoka mare, Larrun, always led away-from marches, even when she changed bands twice. When she came to us she was, for her own, certainly good, reasons terrified of people and always marched off first. Now that she is less frightened, she is not the invariable leader. Whoever starts the away-from march is the one most disturbed. It may be the stallion, whose reactions to threat are heightened.

Drifts are those progressive band displacements or changes of activity that happen gradually until the whole band is in another place or activity. Anyone, including youngsters, can initiate these. The pottokas often search out little patches of grass in the high heather and, as the two-year-olds are more exploratory, they often disappear until the mares, wondering what they have found, follow them. Two-year-olds often precipitate synchronized bouts of lying down, too.

These slower changes of activity, which I am grouping under the same phenomenon as synchrony although they are more staggered than exactly synchronous, are more usually termed social facilitation. One horse rolls, followed by another and another; one youngster starts frisking about and sets off general hilarity; one finds something interesting under a bush and soon others crowd to investigate. Enrique and Mariana, two students cataloguing social interactions in a band, saw two instances when one mare urinated and, on hearing her, two others did too. Do what the others are doing, unless you have particular reasons not to, is a guideline for horses. We, too, are prone to social facilitation in yawning, getting giggling fits,

*Fig. 5.7    Pottoka band in a grazing drift showing directional synchrony.*

*Fig. 5.8    Let's all sit down: an activity often initiated by youngsters. (Photo: Javier Solis)*

and changing mood, but we do not seem to be able to speed it up to the level of mirror-image synchrony or wheeling in formation as horses do. Perhaps our narrower visual field limits us.

Horses invite others to share dyadic synchronous activities like playing or mutual grooming by approaching them in particular ways: jauntily for playing, slouchy and head-on for mutual grooming.

The fact that horses move to synchronize with those behind as well as those in front makes me wonder if this helps understand why stallions lower their heads in such a dramatic way while herding. Any horse can move another with his head at normal height, by flattening his ears and giving a head-thrust. These are not very obvious signals to a horse looking backwards out of the corner of her eye while moving, and if she misses them she is liable to shift over towards the stallion's direction to synchronize with him. Lowering his head changes his appearance so radically, even to a corner-of-the-eye glimpse, that he is obviously not inviting a synchronous move.

Synchrony, like cohesion, is such a prevalent feature of equine social behaviour that we scarcely remark on it. Watch them.

## Collision Avoidance, or Respect for Individual Space

When grazing or marching, horses maintain a minimum space of a little more than a metre between them. They do not enter each other's individual space without preliminary signs, or

*Fig. 5.9 Since synchrony is vitally important, all youngsters practise it in play. Fillies, shown here, do not play-fight like colts, but they do practise synchrony.*

*Fig. 5.10   Resting in a huddle, the members of a pottoka band relax the prohibition on invading others' space, though they prefer some huddling partners to others.*

they get threatened; sometimes they get threatened even when they do make preliminary signs, as do stallions rushing up to court the wrong mare when they smell the urine of one in season. Youngsters cannot learn respect for space from their mothers, whose space they continually invade; they must learn from others, and in the process get threatened more than do adults. They are the only ones in a stampede who do not maintain a space between themselves and their dams.

There are times when horses relax this rule, notably when resting in huddles. Pottokas seek the shadow of a big rock, and Camargue horses respite from horseflies, in these close huddles. In both cases motivation overrides space considerations, and in both arousal is low. Pottokas also huddle when shoving for chestnuts or salt, but two bands never try to do this at once. Within bands or between friends the possibility of relaxing space respect does exist; between bands, never.

## MOTIVATION, DECISIONS AND THE FLIGHT ALGORITHM

The answer to the question of whether the dimmer switch that controls adherence to the flight algorithm ever gets turned off is: no, it doesn't. Its factors are always present, guiding horses in their daily lives as they move together from one activity to another. Individual motivation may override them at times, dictate which horse initiates a change, and influence whether the majority decide to go with the change; but the three factors are always there, ready to be turned up if circumstances warrant. Cohesion and synchrony define the default setting of where and how to be in relation to others.

Horses, then, are constantly aware of each other. Each horse's position, orientation and movement is determined by a balance of two major influences: first, the position, orientation and movement of others in the assembly and second, individual motivation, often prompted by internal needs. What emerges is a composite, coordinated dance in which no individuals direct others but all influence and are influenced by others in a continuous subtle interplay.

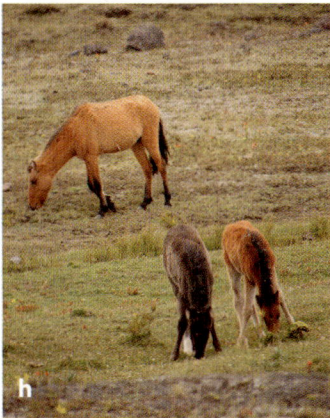

Figs. 5.11a to 5.11i    Step-by step synchrony shown by two foals grazing. Cotopaxi. (Photos: Javier Solis)

Feral horse bands are self-organizing units of autonomous individuals, without leaders or directors.

Does that necessarily imply that all individuals have equal weight in initiating mass decisions? Foals do not: they are adjuncts of their mothers, though an alert, staring foal may alert his mother and the stallion too. Yearlings also get little notice, but two-year-olds already do, although they are still influenced by their mothers in times of trouble. At full independence, after natal dispersal, they are in completely new territory and in a network of new social relations, so they are less likely to make independent decisions that others follow. Mature mares' decisions are influenced not only by motivation and the flight algorithm, but by experience too. The mature brumbies refused to follow the younger mare wanting to go and lick the road until they saw a car pass by with its headlights on: they knew that was the safety signal, and that thereafter they would have early warning of any car approaching. The mature cimarrons in round-up stampedes are the ones who know how to swerve to safety. Larrun knows that people can be nasty. Experience influences their decisions.

Recently, the idea has arisen that in many animal societies there are 'keystone' characters, individuals that influence mass decisions more than do others. It has proved helpful in discovering common traits in such diverse characters as male primates, broker dolphins, nest scouts in honeybee swarms and matriarch elephants. Are there keystone horses?

The stallion seems to be a keystone individual in initiating flight, but horses are perfectly capable of bunching and running away without stallions, so the stallion is not such a key figure as might seem. He is simply more reactive to threat, a characteristic of testosterone. The apparently keystone α mare, as we have seen, is a myth. But if experienced mares as an age-sex class refuse to follow a foolish young mare's decision, she will (usually) come back to maintain cohesion with the band, so band decisions are ultimately unanimous, although based on individual decisions. If there were only one experienced mare, the rest of the band being ready to follow the young one, the stallion would chivvy the reluctant one along too to keep the band together. When two-year-olds leave the band at natal dispersal nobody follows. Since their motivation is high enough to overcome the desire to stay in the band they do not come back and try inviting other members, but wander off without the quality of purposeful, determined movement that invites synchrony.

Bands do not have keystone individuals, but they do contain horses of different ages, sex, motivation and experience: different roles. The male role is to deal with outside threats, from other males, predators or unusual stimuli. A stallion stands out because there is often only one of him in a band, but stallions in multi-male bands and colts line up to evaluate threats too, and may be the first to turn and run, initiating band flight. The mare's role is to feed her foal as best she can, by eating well herself. The youngster's role is to learn. The members of a band have disparate needs that are met by being left alone to complete their roles.

Bourjade (2009) calls band decisions democratic, which they are, but band structure does not correspond to a democracy with an elected, ruling government. It is self-organizing, more akin to some visions of anarchy in which each member's life is his own responsibility to live as he pleases but with the utmost respect for others' need (space) to do the same. No government is necessary, but a common threat to this freedom unites all, as it does in horses. For them, living in society does not represent a struggle against each other, but a united struggle against external enemies – though the devil may take the hindmost who does not attend to the fundamental rules.

## CHAPTER 6

# Interactions

The formula cohere-synchronize-don't collide gives horses a proven guide as to how to escape predators, and they practise it in a more relaxed way in the absence of threat, too. Many fish and birds do the same, going about their lives with an eye on each other and grouping closely when peril looms. But the algorithm does not define how to get a mate, or the composition and size of a band, or how to interact with each other either between or within bands.

## FERAL HORSE SOCIAL ORGANIZATION

Linklater showed that the social groupings of feral horses are remarkably constant whether they live in deserts, on islands, on mountains or marshes, in the tropics or temperate zones. They have natal bands, bachelor bands and sometimes have mixed-sex peer groups. They practise natal dispersal. They have non-defended home ranges but stallions do defend their mares from other males: a polygynous female-defence mating system. Only the constraints of management, apparently, change it.

Having such a fixed strategy is actually rather rare among ungulates, which are notorious for having various strategies – territorial defence, lekking, female-following, roving, maintaining seasonal or permanent harems or mates, to name but a few – and swapping from one to another depending on the environmental circumstances. Horses do not. Although bachelors try to sneak-mate, once they can set up more permanent alliances with mares they settle to defending them whatever the environmental circumstances.

Nevertheless, there are quite striking differences between populations in the closeness of bands and their relations to each other, as the Camoruco cimarrons showed. They also allowed re-interpretation of a number of points, the significance of which is not so clear in other populations.

### The Camoruco Cimarrons

The first time Vanesa and I saw any, fitted the standard picture. Faint from the heat as we explored the savannah on a quad, we parked it to collapse in the threads of shade of a thorn bush, and they came: five of them, skinny, with short tails, jollily jostling along, tossing their heads as they aimed soft bites at each other's chests. One was male – no, two. Three. Surprising how long it can take to see the evidence. They were all males. We had found a bachelor band.

They remind me irresistibly of adolescent boys fooling about: the same lurching shoves,

Fig. 6.1    The Camaruco bands often fuse into a single large herd.

Fig. 6.2    Colts play in the freshness of the dawn, Camarucos. (Photo: Vanesa Ugarte)

Fig. 6.3    Amiguete investigates an investigator, while Bambú (far right) watches.

nudges, mock fights – the graceful, elastic movements distinguish them from real fights, though the moves are the same. Colts aim playful bites at each other's necks, often standing face to face so they seem to be fencing and feinting. They rear up and wave their hooves at each other, finding one leg hooked over the other's withers as he goes for a chest bite. They waltz nose to tail, nipping each other's hind legs, or drop to their knees with their bottoms in the air, still aiming bites at each other's legs. Every few minutes they stop, yawn a couple of times, and throw themselves at each other again. Despite being thin, the Camoruco bachelors seemed to have plenty of surplus energy to waste on these antics, which sometimes went on for as long as half an hour before both strolled off suddenly.

One of them, a little shorter and stockier than the rest, was the blotchy pink and white known as sabino. His head was frankly chestnut, with a broad blaze, the upper part almost as wide as his broad forehead, and a white throat. He seemed particularly friendly to all, nibbling their faces and rubbing his neck against theirs. This handsome chap, whom I grew to love dearly, we called Amiguete, little friend.

When they realized we were there, they shot off in a horror that still had a tinge of mockery about it, high-tailing and dancing about once they had put a decent distance between us and them.

The second day provided the shock. We found the whole herd grazing peacefully together.

Nothing that I had read about or seen in feral horses had led me to expect to see so many horses close together in an apparently homogeneous herd: 142, not including twenty-four foals. We stared in disbelief. Worse, they all had the short, hock-length tails that usually distinguish yearlings, so we could only guess their ages.

At first we could distinguish no bands at all, but little by little the situation became clearer. We picked out our original bachelor band, moving together round the outskirts of the herd. Another little band, two mares with two small males, kept some thirty metres apart from the others, and yet another stayed further away. But in the main mass thirteen obviously mature stallions wandered about freely, occasionally greeting each other, and did not appear to be attached to any mares in particular. There were more, younger males within the herd too.

One stallion in particular stood out: a chunky black horse with a broad blaze, whose greying cheeks, white patches on the sides of his tail and stiff movements revealed old age. Bambú seemed a central reference point for the whole herd. When he stared at us, other stallions stopped what they were doing and stared too; when he relaxed, so did they. His relations with all the others were particularly friendly.

Over the years that we studied this herd, with its yearly changes brought about deaths and youngsters reaching maturity, we found them all together on more than half the days we saw them. Sometimes a band would detach itself; sometimes the herd split into two or three large groups; occasionally, the bands were completely separate, though almost always in sight of each other. Even when the herd was together there were always two or three bands that stayed at least thirty to fifty metres distant: the bands with novice stallions (those who have been bachelors the year before); those of small, weak stallions who formed allegiances

Fig. 6.4    Amiguete, in his second year as stallion, leads his band. At right, little Oreja, with an equally undergrown helper. Between them they have two mares, both behind Amiguete's band.

to maintain any mares at all; natal bands whose stallion was sick tend to be separate too. In that first year, the two-stallion band included a lame little bay stallion and a light sabino so tiny we thought him a yearling. He had lost his mother as a foal and never grew. One ear drooped, probably as a result of infection caused by tick infestation, so we called him Oreja (Ear). Oreja's fortunes changed over the years. Some years he was with the bachelors, always playing, but some years he was a stallion with a mare or two, and sometimes recruited a helper too. He always kept them separate from the main mass; in fact Guapo (Handsome) once chased his little band off when they neared the big herd.

Some stallions also separated their mares from the main mass for a few days when one was in season. This operation made quite clear that mares choose their stallions, rather than stallions dominating or owning mares. Moving into a mass of horses, the stallion lowered his head into the driving position. Most ignored him, but a mare here, another there, and a third over yonder started to move hurriedly, followed by their foals or yearlings. They had not been next to each other but dispersed among others, so the stallion had no definite bunch to aim for. He simply gave the signal and they chose to listen to him, emerging out of the mass together in a cohesive band. This is not the impression given in most feral populations, when the stallions seem to oblige their mares to remain grouped and separated from others, although they cannot prevent one from leaving if she is bent on it. But the Camoruco herd showed clearly that the mares are with a stallion because they want to be with him, and he is there to be with them.

An alternative hypothesis might be that the in-season mare recognized that the stallion was driving her and that the others chose to go with her because of the bonds between them. This did not seem to be the case because the mares did not stay together when in the main mass. Moreover, the mare in question might be a young one, to whom the others could not be firmly bonded.

Bands did sometimes wander away from the main herd for no discernible reason, too. When that happened we took the opportunity to identify each member carefully. While the smaller bands were constant, the bigger ones tended to fluctuate, with some constant members and some floaters who joined them some days but not others.

When the herd was all together, the space it occupied was seldom round, or defined by an area of good grazing as on Cotopaxi, but oval or cigar-shaped. Stallions tended to take up

*Fig. 6.5    Jotero herding. Four mares respond to his signal but the others ignore him: he is not their stallion.*

typical positions: Careto in the middle, Jotero at the end, for instance. Analysis of neighbours showed that bands were not randomly ordered, but that some were neighbours more often than not. When the herd split into two or more large sub-herds, we found the same preferences. Only years more analysis could show whether stallions prefer the company of others from the same bachelor group, or natal group, or whether mares affect the distribution. In elephants the same tendency for certain bands to fuse and then separate is seen, and is called fission-fusion.

What we saw, then, is that there were defined natal bands, although we found it difficult to distinguish them, and that they usually lived happily mixed together except when special circumstances made the stallions prefer to keep them separate: novice stallions, weak or sick ones or those that had mares in season, that rejoined the mass when oestrus had passed. The norm was living together.

## Stallion Tolerance in Different Feral Populations

In the different feral populations I have seen, there are marked differences in the tolerance that stallions show to each other. At one extreme are the brumbies, whose bands were never in sight of each other and had clear home ranges. The stallions marked paths with large dung piles: dung piles with history, for they were clearly used for months on end. I saw the brumbies in mid-winter, when stallions are usually more relaxed about letting their bands spread out.

*Fig. 6.6   Pottoka stallions Pintxo (left) and Ekain, here beginning the dungpile ritual. Pintxo still shows high emotional tension.*

The pottoka bands seldom meet, and when they do the stallions usually go through the sniffing, squealing, prancing and dunging ritual, although they know perfectly well who each other is, before stationing themselves between their bands and each other. They, too, have home ranges although these overlap, and they make large, historic dung piles.

The Cotopaxi bands often grazed together in the same places, at first glance appearing to be a large herd of fifty or sixty horses, although a knowing eye could distinguish the bands (*see* Fig. 3.3). Usually the distance between bands was greater than the distance between

*Fig. 6.7    The Torres del Paine bagual herd, which never splits up into bands.*

the members of a band, so there was a narrow strip of no-man's-land between each band. However some bands did intermingle, sometimes for hours or days on end. Almost invariably these bands had two stallions, and the stallions from both bands greeted each other amicably. The only exception was what appeared to be a two-stallion band with five mares and a few youngsters. A foal startled at a passing car, alerting his mother and then one stallion, who stepped forth, staring. All the others bunched and ran away together, but after a few metres some mares came back to the staring stallion, while the remainder ran on with the other: another example of the fact that mares are with their stallion from choice rather than as a result of his control. On subsequent days we found these two bands separate.

These Cotopaxi horses' home ranges overlapped so much that our attempts at mapping them are almost impossible to decipher. One male would dung on another's fresh dung, or in ritual meeting, but they did not make large, historic dung piles. Between-band stallion meetings were more likely to be friendly than in the pottokas.

The Camoruco cimarrons' bands all had exactly the same home range, or rather, there are places where all bands go and others that none go. Like the Cotopaxi horses, they did not make large dung piles.

The cimarrons' preferences might be thought to be a result of living within an enclosure, but it is as big or bigger than the area of some islands where bands are discrete. The Patagonian baguales, who have limitless space and roam far, behave the same. Victor Moraga has

*Fig. 6.8   In Tierra del Fuego similar baguales, in similar country but without puma, live in separate bands. Behind them, guanaco.*

visited them regularly over years and has never seen discrete bands, though that does not mean that they do not exist in the sense that mares attach themselves to one particular stallion, as we see in the cimarrons. Careful analysis of interactions and nearest neighbours would provide answers, but given a close-packed, homogenous herd of 100, with few colour variations, the task is difficult.

Table 1 summarizes the differences.

**Table 1    Characteristics of Different Feral Populations.**

| Population | No. | Habitat | Seasons | Predation | Band distance | Fusion | Home range | Dung piles | Dynamics |
|---|---|---|---|---|---|---|---|---|---|
| Brumbies | 70 | Mountain wood, open valleys | Hot dry snow | Slight | 1k m + | No | Separate | Yes | ? |
| Pottokas | 34 | Mountain wood | Hot dry snow | No | 150m | No | Overlap | Yes | Growing |
| Cotopaxi | 180 | Páramo | None | No | 30m | Some | Much overlap | No | Growing |
| Llanos | 145 | Savannah | Very hot dry floods | Yes | 30m if at all | Yes | All the same | No | Static |
| Baguales | 120 | Mountain wood, open valley | Warm very cold snow | Heavy | None | Always | All the same | No | Losing |

Why should such differences in tolerance exist? Three possibilities suggest themselves: predators, landscape, and climate.

*Predators – or landscape?*

Unlike most feral horses nowadays, the cimarrons live with predators. They all bunch together to flee, and between puma (real or imaginary) and *llaneros* they stampede so often that staying close together most of the time makes sense. I thought this an attractive hypothesis until I read Rubenstein (1986) on plains zebra, which have the same social organization as horses. He found that some populations form big herds while others do not, but that whether they were predated or not was not what made the difference: that depended on the type of terrain they lived in. On open plains, they form herds; where there are clumps of trees and the country is more uneven, they live in separate bands.

The Venezuelan *llanos* fall into the open plain category; but so does the Cotopaxi *páramo*, where bands are more distinguishable and a big, united herd does not form. The Patagonian baguales also live all together all the time, but in wild mountains with wooded slopes and lush valley meadows, not unlike the terrain in which the brumbies stayed strictly separate, except that the mountains are bigger. These baguales are heavily predated by puma, which have increased enormously in numbers since puma hunting was banned in the National Park, on the borders of which the horses live. Patagonian puma are huge beasts. We nearly collided with one feasting on a freshly-killed guanaco, a sobering experience. The predation-leads to-living-together hypothesis gained credibility, despite Rubenstein.

A park ranger had seen the baguales some three weeks earlier and counted seventeen foals. When we saw them there was one, only a couple of days old. We found the rest, one after another, pathetic little dismembered bodies cached in the dense trees bordering the valley meadows. In the long grass you could see where the puma had rushed out at horses grazing only metres away, made its kill and dragged the dead foal back to a stash in the trees. Why were the baguales so stupid as to graze so close to danger, when the valleys were wide and rich enough to graze safely in the middle? (For that matter, why was I, at 54kg, so stupid as to go poking about in the larder of a 90kg puma?) The Venezuelan cimarrons, with poorer grazing, give a wide margin to places with cover for puma.

These baguales are not relics of the original large bagual population, which was wiped out in the 1920s and 1930s by meat traders, but the result of a mass escape from nearby ranches in the 1990s. They multiplied when puma were scarcer, and seem doomed to extinction unless they develop better defence tactics against puma. There was only one yearling, too (curiously, from the mare who had the foal: perhaps she was the only wise mother there), so multiplication has stopped. Is it possible that they have developed an unusual social organization because of puma danger at the same time as not developing the simple tactic of avoiding places where puma are? You could argue that the two behaviours are independent, but selection pressure for one means selection pressure for the other too. But the predator hypothesis seems weakened.[27]

*Patterns of interaction between stallions*
The baguales did, however, show behaviour that the Camoruco cimarrons did not. Despite living together, the stallions had tiffs like normal feral stallions, pawing and biting each other for a few seconds, or flying furiously at a bachelor who had come too close to a mare. The males had marks, scars, little wounds like any other feral male. The cimarrons did not. They were all immaculate.

One of the most striking things about the cimarron males was their lack of aggression towards each other and indeed the friendliness of their social contacts. We have a list of behaviours seen in social contacts. On the friendly (affiliative) side are: friendly approach (ears forward, relaxed gait), nasal contact without tension, neck-rubbing, play, soft nasal contacts to the other's body and sharing individual space. On the conflictive or agonistic (aggressive-defensive: you usually cannot tell which is which) side are: ears back, head-thrust, stamp, squeal, arch neck, passage, rear, charge, bite, kick, ritual dunging. We have a category for 'fight' but we never saw one except a brief rearing and biting tiff during a mass march in 2011, an unusually conflictive year (more later on 2011). We also listed whether, at the time of the contact, either stallion had a mare in season.

Just over half of male-male contacts, whether between two stallions or between a stallion and a bachelor, were purely friendly. The two might simply meet while strolling about and salute each other; they might be two who habitually lived in the same part of the herd, and

*Fig. 6.9    Even pottoka stallions are capable of friendly greeting once they know each other.*

greeted each other often; they might be two who were far apart but raised their heads at the same instant, rushed at each other with an urgency that seemed to spell trouble, greeted each other effusively, played for a few minutes and returned to where they came from.

Agonistic encounters almost invariably involved one stallion stepping in front of another who was wandering about; the first arched his neck, stamping and squealing. The second stallion always stopped. He might go away, or he might stop for a couple of seconds before greeting the challenger. Usually his greeting was accepted and the tension died down, to the extent that friendly head-wrestling and a little play followed (half of the meetings that started with conflictive signals ended with affiliative ones); but the challenger did not move from his position or let the other pass. If, on the other hand, the intruder did not go away or defuse the situation with a polite greeting, the challenger repeated his stamping and squealing; he might move up and down an imaginary line, as if delimiting an invisible boundary, with high, exaggerated steps and ritual dunging. We never saw these encounters escalate into fights with physical contact.

Almost invariably (96 per cent of times) the challenging stallion had a mare obviously in season, or we saw him covering or courting that day or the next. He was protecting his mating rights. As in-season mares leave their scent everywhere as they graze, any stallion might follow the trail, only to find his way blocked by her own stallion.

We did not find that size, age or the particular individual affected the outcome of these encounters. One day it might be G who stopped H, the next vice versa. It depended on who had a mare to defend. One notable encounter took place when Ramón, then a novice stallion with two mares, was grazing some fifty metres from a large group. Humo (Smoke), a grand, mature black stallion, the biggest horse in the herd, suddenly left the group and walked in a determined way towards the little band. Ramón, who was tiny, left his mares and stepped out towards Humo. He looked like David confronting Goliath. Timidly, screwing his courage to the limit, he gave a little stamp and squeaked a warning. Humo stopped, bent down and gave his head a rub and went away. Humo could have eaten Ramón alive, but respected his signals.

In other feral horses, including the pottokas, these encounters would almost invariably be more dramatic, with rears and foreleg strikes, most especially if one stallion had a mare in season. Our cimarrons, though, reduced all conflict to an interchange of signals that others invariably respect, even when one was a strong, mature stallion and the other a small novice.

*Effects of climate*
Why did the cimarrons behave like this? The best guess, for me, is the winter. Almost all deaths occur in the winter floods. Any animal not in good shape at the end of April is missing the next year. We found their bleached bones out on the savannah, but there was not even enough hair to guess their coat colour or identify them. The winter floods bring innumerable bacteria and parasites I had not even heard of, apart from clouds of various biting, chewing, blood-sucking flies. A horse with an open wound, no matter how small, is vulnerable to infection. In 2011 we had the disgusting experience of watching an unfortunate bachelor become infected and die, slowly and agonizingly, from pitium, a water-borne parasite that enters broken skin, in this case in the whorl in the ventral mid-line of the belly where little flies often make a sore. Gradually what was originally an invisible lesion became a vast open wound dripping pus, until he died. A horse with an open wound does not survive the winter floods.

Natural selection is pitiless but effective. It has in this case eliminated any horse liable to violent action, selecting the peace-makers who reduce tiffs to mere signals. Since they use and respect these minimal signals, they can live together in a big herd in a way that other feral horses cannot.

Noticeably, the Cotopaxi stallions also had few conflictive meetings and many friendly ones, though they do not have the climatic problems of the cimarrons. Despite being wrapped in damp, windy cloud half the time the *páramo* is so high as to be pest-free and there are now no predators. Perhaps different populations have different reasons for maintaining distance or not.

In different populations, summer can also be influential on behaviour. In the middle of the day in summer, groups of up to a hundred semi-feral Camargue ponies, comprising many natal bands, huddle together without any conflict between the stallions. Duncan and Vigne (1979) showed that in these giant huddles, the horses receive fewer horsefly bites than when in smaller groups or separated. This behaviour does not seem to correspond to that of the cimarrons, who were together but not in a huddle; moreover at the times we saw them there were very few horseflies. Nevertheless it does show that stallions are prepared to allow other stallions to rest near their mares if such behaviour benefits them, as this temporary mutual truce does.

Thus, although the natal band and bachelor band pattern is universal in horses, they do modify home range sizes, nearness of groups, and marking or warning behaviour. Since most studies do not give data on tolerance I have only a small sample to go on, but no unifying factor is yet obvious.

## POPULATION DYNAMICS

Some figures on the Camoruco cimarron herd will help round out the picture of their social life and its pressures. For four years the population remained stable at around 142–146 individuals, not counting that season's foals. This corresponds well with Dr Vargas' estimate of 150, the number his grandfather left as feral; he saw the same number on limiting them to their present pasture in 1997. Most feral populations grow at a rate of between 10 per cent and 30 per cent every year except where starvation limits numbers, as on small islands. Here, starvation is not the problem: disease, parasites and puma are.

Generally, the population consists of fourteen to sixteen stallions, twenty to twenty-five bachelors, and around fifty breeding mares. The remainder are yearlings, two year-olds of both sexes, and fillies who have not yet bred. They rarely produce a foal before the age of four; more usually they are five. In contrast, my pottokas foal at three or, in some cases, two.

The average year's foal crop was twenty-five: mares did not foal every year but in alternate years, continuing to suckle yearlings. This low fecundity is unusual for criollos: one study gave nearly 80 per cent fecundity, but the horses lived in less marginal conditions. Stress, as measured by faecal cortisol concentration, decreases fertility. Our cimarrons certainly experience climatic stress, on top of chronic anaemia-producing diseases and blood-sucking flies. Moreover the land is extremely acid (ph value 4.5–5), so that calcium, vital for good milk production and bone formation, is scarce. Producing a healthy foal in these conditions seems little short of miraculous.

On average 17 per cent, or one in six, foals did not survive until the next year. A few died before the winter, some as a result of a stampede that left them behind, easy pickings for puma. Foals born late, in April, were not strong enough to survive the floods. However, if they survived that first winter, their chances of living to twenty-five or so (judging by the teeth of skeletons) were high. Young males have a higher mortality rate than fillies: notice that the figures above give thirty-eight males to fifty females. Some of this shortfall may have been due to the removal of bachelors for ranch work, though this stopped before our studies began. Berger noticed the same in mustangs and concluded that it might be a consequence of injuries sustained in fighting: a kick in the face can result in a broken tooth and septicaemia.[28] But our cimarrons did not fight.

Horses destined to die in the winter often showed symptoms of advanced trypanosomiasis: muscle wastage and ataxia (lack of coordination) in the hindquarters. We also found two skeletons, both females around twenty years old, with tremendous breaks in one molar and bone degeneration in the mandible beneath. Normally the teeth, even in aged skeletons, were in good order. There are no stones in the *llanos* but the horses do sometimes eat nuts that could break teeth.

### 2011, a difficult year

The year 2011 was catastrophic for the cimarrons. There was a plague of ticks, and they carried Babesia (piroplasmosis). We found twenty-six bodies, twenty mares and six males. Usually we did not find bodies: horses died in the winter, and all we found were bones picked clean during the floods by, amongst others, the scavenger crabs whose own skeletons pepper the plain. Bodies mean they have died in the summer, which is highly unusual. Of the mares, fifteen were seventeen years old or more. There are two strains of Babesia, one usually fatal while the other is not so severe. Possibly the disproportionate number of aged mares indicates that this was the less lethal strain, but that they were already debilitated by other chronic infections. Most unusually, five were amongst the trees of Flor Amarillo, Flor Blanca and el Camaruco. These were all mares. Near them were three foals eaten by puma, unlike the two little bodies out on the savannah not far from mares' corpses, which bore no signs of violence. The horses always avoided the deep shade of the trees, probably precisely because of the puma danger; vampire bats also roost there. We found one very sick mare hiding in the shade; she died two days later. These horses seemed to have been driven into the cool by the torture of high fever.

Normally only one or two horses died in the summer, and we counted ourselves unlucky to witness death; but three more died during our stay.

Curiously, there was a disproportionate number of pale-coloured horses among the dead. Normally about a quarter of the herd were pale coloured: grey, cream (*capino*), sabino or light dun, the rest being black (few, with a strong family resemblance), chestnut, bay or a chestnut with black in the mane and tail that, for ease of identification amongst ourselves, we call *camoruco*. Nearly three-quarters of the dead horses were pale, mostly cream or light dun. The *llaneros* dislike pale horses: they say they are weaker, by which they mean more likely to die.

The severity of the tick infestation was shown by the number of tick-eating birds we saw. Normally in a month's watching we see a *caricari*, a hawk-like bird, picking ticks from the mane of a horse for ten minutes or so on one or two days. In 2011 there were two or three every day, constantly working, joined by the smaller *garrapatero* (tickbird). Once, a *caricari* had his head sunk deep into a mare's ear, flapping his wings in her face to keep his position while she tilted her head to help him reach deeper.

Many of the stallions we had watched for years had disappeared without trace: big black Humo, the friends Lazan and Guapo, long-maned Elegante and Jotero the dancer. We found the bodies of little Ramón, only in his second year as stallion and eight years old, and playful Oreja, who was fourteen; towards the end of our stay both the golden palomino Dorado and young Padrote ('Stallion') were clearly dying.

Every year we had arrived to find a couple of established stallions missing, their mares redistributed, and a couple of novice stallions starting their breeding careers. To lose half the stallions in one year meant serious social disturbance and previously unconceivable opportunities for bachelors.

This social upheaval was further complicated by the mules. In 2010 there was a mass escape from the ranch of five four-year-old mules, who joined the cimarrons. Four were entire males. There was also a three-year-old male mule born in the herd, out of a mare who had escaped already pregnant. Male mules are, though infertile, nothing short of sex maniacs. In 2011 they attacked the stallions, ran the mares off, raped them mercilessly and, worst of all, would not let the stallions mate. Whenever they saw a stallion mount a mare they ran full tilt into him so he fell off before finishing. One had started this behaviour already in 2010, harassing Humo's mares and stealing two, always the same two. Humo would retrieve them but the mule came too, only to repeat the performance. After three weeks of continuous patience, Humo finally lost his temper and attacked the mule, rearing up at him, biting and kicking furiously until the mule left. We cheered. These stallions, then, can attack and fight effectively, though in normal circumstances they choose to resolve conflicts symbolically.

Naturally, the mules did not respect the stallions' polite signals. Nor did the double-barrelled kicks delivered repeatedly by frightened mares have any effect on them. They seemed to think it was a stimulating chest massage. When a mare was exhausted, the mule raped her, repeating the performance only minutes later. Despite the mares' squeals and the drum-

*Fig. 6.10    The mule Escopeta (Shotgun) kicks and pushes Chocolate off the mare he is covering.*

beat of their kicks the stallions never came to their rescue, though a mare did attack a mule attempting to rape her yearling daughter and succeeded in defeating him.

One mule held a harem of six mares, as if he were a normal stallion with a natal band. He seemed to have taken them from Amiguete. Since they did not appreciate his company he had to work ceaselessly to keep them together. But mules are tireless.

This constant disruption, with squealing mares and hectic chases almost daily, had an effect on social relations between the males. The number of friendly contacts diminished and the agonistic ones increased. The only physical conflict we have seen occurred in 2011, a brief rearing and pawing episode during a mass march. Instead of forming a mixed group, the bands tended to be strung out in a line, with the stallions marking limits between bands.

Social stress increases conflict behaviour even in feral horses, a factor that is widely ignored in domestic horses (*see* Chapter 7).

There were only six foals when we arrived, instead of the usual twenty-five or so. Three more were born, but three died. Whether the mules had anything to do with this lack of foals I do not know for sure, but suspect so. Rape in the early months of pregnancy causes abortion. During Humo's mule problems in 2010 there was a young foal in his band. Because of the constant galloping to and fro we only once, in twenty-six days of observation, saw him suckle, and he got very little rest too. Probably, then, the mules did not help foal survival at all. Certainly they affected the 2012 foal crop, which we did not see.

When we left, there were 117 cimarrons and six foals, two of which looked poorly.

Worse was to come, though we did not see it. The floods were exceptionally heavy (global warming) and mortality was high. But all the mules died. The *llaneros* say that when mules enter deep water they stop, unlike horses, who keep going.

What we had seen is that normally this population does not increase, but holds its own. Whether it will manage to overcome this huge loss remains to be seen.[29]

## INDIVIDUAL SUCCESS IN FERAL BAND

### Survival

Who survives in these harsh circumstances? Who lives to breed offspring to carry a horse's genetic heritage into the future? For the cimarrons, disease, parasites and puma are life's main hazards. Luckier feral horses do not face these challenges, and many populations like the pottokas breed at an alarming rate, increasing up to 30 per cent per year, a problem in itself. On islands, sheer starvation limits life. We are used to the idea that only the fittest survive, but does that necessarily mean out-competing others of the same species and population?

### Competition for Control over Maintenance Resources?

Among the cimarrons the idea is absurd. There is food for all, although after the long, hot summer it is of such poor quality that the horses are thin, despite eating almost continually. There are no better or worse home ranges. Water just gets shallower. The cimarrons do not rest in shade, but out in the most open parts of the savannah, where puma may be spotted from far off.

*Fig. 6.11   Competing for a focal resource, salt, the pottoka band shows no aggression: they push and shove.*

In most other feral populations the same is true. Resources are so widely spread that there is no competition for them, though some unusual situations exist where whole bands displace others for rare resources. One was Miller's queue for desert water, where big bands displaced smaller ones; another was Rubenstein's small patch of good grazing on an overpopulated island. In both cases, competition was not between the individuals of one band but between whole bands benefiting from the relative strengths of their stallions. Where grazing is poor, as it is in the winter for most feral horses, the individuals in a band spread out, avoiding possible competition (Berger 1986, Kaseda 1983).

The pottokas, though, do occasionally find focal resources (goodies at one spot) of two types that could provoke within-band competition. The cowman leaves salt blocks for his cattle, and the chestnut pickers sort their crop into marketable and reject chestnuts, turning the rejects out in small heaps outside their plantations. When a band finds one of these focal resources, the pottokas do not compete aggressively: they simply push and shove each other in an eager crowd. Only once have I seen any aggression, when Hodei the black stallion was standing apart licking earth while the rest of the band was shoving to lick another spot. Twice in half an hour youngsters approached him. At one he laid his ears back; at the other he showed a hind foot. The youngsters went back to shoving. Hodei was thin, so perhaps he was particularly motivated about the salty earth. Normally he shoved along with the rest.

When a thirsty feral band reaches water, they do not aggress each other either: they shove, as Stevens (1988) saw when she restricted the water supply on an island. This does mean that the biggest ones get their share first, but since they are the mature, lactating mares they need it more. In natural situations horses do not come across limited, focal resources where competition between the individuals of a band might affect their survival.

## Male Competition for Mares

Where competition does exist in this generally egalitarian society is between males for mares, since one stallion suffices for up to eight or ten, although three or four are more usual numbers. What is at stake for a stallion is his capacity to propagate his genes: that is, to have healthy foals who survive to reproduce. This does not depend entirely on how many mares he has, although that is certainly a factor.

The first problem for a male, is of course, developing into a stallion. In other populations this depends on being awake to opportunities, on stealing coverings or mares, or as a final resort, on fighting. We never saw cimarron bachelors trying to steal mares or coverings. (The pottokas do try, but have never been seen to succeed.)

The cimarron bachelors had two strategies, one of which has not been described before. We called them Latin Kings or Moles.

Latin Kings lived in bachelor bands, of which there were sometimes two or three, with up to seven individuals. This is the normal pattern in feral horses. They spent an immense amount of time playing or in gentler friendly social contact, moving round the bands or the main mass constantly. Sometimes they indulged in their most dramatic play-bouts right next to a natal band, as if trying to catch the eye of a filly.

Play-fights have various fixed components mentioned earlier: neck-wrestling, kneeling, rearing and waltzing. They also include sexual elements like mounting or following another bachelor nipping at his hocks. Mounting is not very efficient since the one underneath bounces and kicks playfully, but it does at least teach them which end to get on: sexual orientation in

*Fig. 6.12    Latin Kings playing, pottoka style. If this were a real fight, their ears would be flat back.*

*Fig. 6.13    Pintxo, in his bachelor days, plays with young stallion Ibai. Right, Ibai's mare Txori and their daughter Serrana.*

*Fig. 6.14   Typical beginner's inadequate mount.  Although the filly Urduri is willing, Oihan's practice mounts in play with his fellow bachelors have taught him to keep clear of back legs.*

ethological terms does not refer to sex preference but to posture. In mammals the sex act is learned.[30] Play is a great teacher of all social and sexual behaviour, but a slight drawback for horses is that, since their playmates kick when mounted, they tend to keep too far away from their first mares' back-end when mounting, and have to learn again to keep closer.

Play is generally considered to be practice of the elements that are important in an adult's behaviour: for kittens, stalking and pouncing; for dogs, chasing and biting; for rabbits, running and hiding. However, the bachelors are mainly practising a pattern that they will never use: fighting. Why?

When a filly leaves her natal band, she generally joins the bachelors. One might expect turmoil: five eager young males and a willing female. There is no trouble. She makes friends with all, and they go around in a band together, playing and flirting like young teenagers for what may be days or weeks. Little by little, one bachelor starts to place himself between the filly and his friends, cutting off her contacts with them. Day by day they are a little more separated from the band until one day they are far away, a young couple starting another natal band. However, this does not mean that the new stallion breaks all his ties with his erstwhile friends: from time to time he leaves his bride and goes off to play with them before returning to her, if she is still around.

The function of play-fighting, here at least, is not to practise fighting but to avoid it: during their play, they have already found out who would win if it did come to a fight. There is a

Fig. 6.15   *A group of bachelors (from left to right Elegante, Padrote, Joropo, Ramón) joined by a grey filly. Eventually she paired up with Amiguete (far left, grazing), who thus became a novice stallion.*

distinct parallel between their play and the horseplay (!) of adolescent boys, especially in street gangs, who similarly avoid confrontations with the boys they have found stronger or more agile while wrestling playfully. For boys and bachelor horses the same rule applies: in play, nobody gets hurt. If one plays too roughly for the other, the second leaves and refuses to play with him.

### An unusual conflict

Only once did we see any conflict in this competitive situation, and it seemed to be the result of mistaken identity. A filly in season, followed by a donkey (there were two in the herd but they were too small to cover the mares) joined a bachelor band. One bachelor wanted to separate her from the others, but it did not occur to him to cover her. A second wanted to cover her, and she was only too willing, but it did not occur to him to separate her from the others. She was taken away repeatedly, only to dash back to the band and her hopeful suitor. We laughed for hours at the ludicrous situation as it repeated itself again and again. There was no ill-humour in the situation: the younger bachelors were all playing.

Not far off was a novice stallion, Padrote, who had been with the bachelors the year before, acquired a sabino mare and now had a foal out of her. She was some thirty metres to the right of Padrote, whose attention was attracted by the rumpus as the wrangling bachelors drew near from the left. Coincidentally, the bachelors' filly was also sabino, not a usual colour. Padrote stared at them fixedly, then charged flat-out into the middle of the band, delivering bites left and right as he drove the filly away. The bachelors all took this as another jolly game and joined in, but Padrote was deadly serious. He launched savage bites at them as they galloped in parallel; once, he stopped, reared and flailed his forelegs at another, who hastily withdrew. As they realized Padrote was not playing, they dropped out one by one until only the would-be separator stayed with them. All this took place at full-tilt gallop, the filly trying to turn back into the others rather than out-run Padrote. Finally, even the last bachelor dropped out, leaving only the filly, fleeing as fast as she could, and the donkey.

*Fig. 6.16   Padrote attacks one of the bachelors that appear to have stolen his mare. The filly that caused the conflict is the middle horse of the threesome; the other two are bachelors. Padrote's own mare and foal are grazing peacefully to the right.*

About a hundred metres away was a large composite group grazing. The filly flew towards them and into them, but Padrote would not let her stop so she shot out the other side again, leaving a puzzled stallion gazing after them. She bolted for another group, almost flattening a foal who was lying asleep, with the same result. Finally she spotted us, sitting in a group, and flew towards us for safety. At only about thirty metres away she realized that we were not horses, and stopped. She, Padrote and the donkey gazed at us for several minutes until Padrote's real mare, missing him, neighed. Exhausted, they all walked towards her. They had been galloping hard for over forty minutes.

And Padrote now had two mares, both sabino. Our interpretation of this unusual event was that he thought the bachelors had stolen his mare.

### The Latin King ploy

After laying claim to a filly that appeared in a bachelor band, a Latin King kept her separate from the main block, though the next year their band, which another mare had usually joined, was once again integrated with the others. Usually the second mare was not a filly; characteristically she was no great prize either, but thin, or a bit lame: a mare who perhaps was not very interesting to a more mature stallion, and chose protection where she could. Often she had a foal or yearling with her.

### Moles

The second bachelor strategy we saw was that of a Mole. Moles lived within natal bands whose stallions let them. Both Dorado and Elegante had up to four or five Moles in their bands and were very friendly with them, often playing with them. None of these Moles was the son of the stallion in whose band he lived. Unlike the ostentatious Latin Kings, Moles kept a low profile and could often be seen grazing close to one of the stallion's daughters. When their band merged with others, they 'Moled about', making friends with other fillies too. Since they did not advertise their presence, the stallions tolerated them.

In 2011, when there were no fewer than seven new stallions, we were interested to see that the ex-Moles did not separate their bands from others, as do ex-Latin Kings. One band was accompanied by two brothers, the Nicos (Nicolás and Nicordón), while another, invariably next door, was held by the third almost identical Nico Lucero. (They are all a dark, rich dun,

Fig. 6.17    The stallion Dorado plays with one of his moles. (Photo: Vanesa Ugarte)

Fig. 6.18
Two of
Dorado's
moles
playing: note
that their
ears aren't
flattened.
(Photo:
Vanesa
Ugarte)

distinguished only by facial markings that you cannot always see, so we had earlier called them all Nico.) All three Nicos had been with Dorado the year before.

To sum up: the Latin King strategy is to arrive at the outskirts of a natal band with a flourish and fandango, attracting the eye of any filly ready to leave the band. However, this also attracts the eye of the stallion, who may drive them away or, more often, parade up and down high-stepping, arching his neck and marking the line with his dung. The Mole strategy is not to attract any attention but, acting completely innocent, to insinuate himself among other bands and quietly establish relations with fillies before returning to his own band, in which he may have a potential mate anyway.

Moles may be a speciality of our cimarrons, because they are not described in any other studies, although Linklater mentions New Zealand bands with 'up to four or five' males. Whether these are bachelor bands joined by a filly or Mole-infested natal bands is not made clear. In Elegante's case his natal band evolved from a bachelor band that more and more mares joined without his separating them from the bachelors; he had all the mating rights, some bachelors left and others arrived until none of the originals remained. Dorado was a fully mature stallion whom bachelors joined as youngsters.

The following extraordinary behaviour, which we witnessed four times, has never been described. A Mole courts and mounts a mare in the same band. She is in season, in fact in her foal heat since she has a new foal at foot. Seeing the Mole on top, the stallion approaches, fast. The Mole hurriedly dismounts but does not go away. The stallion smells the mare, who at this point is usually urinating, performs Flehmen, shows no interest and goes away, leaving the Mole to mount the mare again. Often he actually gives the Mole a friendly greeting. The Mole's mounting is inadequate: he does not come close enough to the mare to achieve full intromission, or he is clumsy, badly-placed or loses his balance.

Twice the stallion was Dorado, twice Elegante. The Moles were different each time.

Why should a mature, experienced stallion allow an unrelated bachelor to mount an in-season mare? The only explanation I can think of relates to the low fertility of the mares. In good conditions a mare conceives in her foal heat, ten to twelve days after foaling, or in her subsequent heat. But our cimarron mares did not breed every year. Therefore, even if they showed oestrus behaviour (and in all cases the mare was in her foal heat) they were probably not ovulating, for they did not become pregnant. Oestrus behaviour without ovulation is quite possible: indeed it is normal for native mares living where the seasons are very marked, as in Britain, to show oestrus in the winter without ovulating. In the *llanos* the day-length is always the same, but the mares may be so deprived of protein that they cannot ovulate so soon after birth, when they are also lactating. An experienced stallion recognizes non-ovulatory oestrus: he may not cover the mare at all even though she solicits him, or if he does so it is in a desultory fashion, often not achieving ejaculation (at least that is what I have seen in my own four pasture-breeding stallions). Probably she is not producing enough pheromone to excite him fully. However, a bachelor has never mounted, or even been allowed near, an in-season mare. Even a lesser quantity of pheromone excites him enough to mount, although it is significant that his mounting is inadequate and incomplete.

Therefore my reading of the situation is this: when the stallion saw the Mole covering the mare, he rushed over to prevent him from so doing. On performing Flehmen, he realized that the mare was not ovulating and went away. In every case the stallion did not perform Flehmen repeatedly as he would do in normal courtship and mounting, building up his libido, but only once.

Possibly Moles' alliances with immature fillies affected the fillies' choice of mate when they were ready, but we did not have enough data to show whether this is true.

*Death of the band stallion*

Another way of gaining mares, whatever the bachelor's strategy, is as a result of stallions dying. Novice stallions (Bambino was one) sometimes appeared with two, three or even four mares, complete with foals or yearlings that had previously been with a now-disappeared stallion. Since death usually occurs in the winter we did not see the process but it is unlikely, in view of the lack of marks, that any physical conflict took place. What we did see is that when a stallion was ill his band was always very far from the others.

In 2011 when Dorado was clearly in a terminal decline he had four Moles in his band. One was the sorry creature that died of pitium. Another was a particularly glorious big chestnut with white spots on his face and neck and splodges on his sides who looked as if someone had thrown a glass of milk at him, so we called him Vaso de Leche. He joined Dorado's band as a two-year-old in 2008 and was a special favourite of Dorado, who often touched, rubbed and played with him. As Dorado sickened, Vaso de Leche gradually took over the role of stallion. When they rested (particularly close together, unusually huddled) Vaso de Leche's head could be seen high above them: he, not Dorado, was the band's main vigilant. On the march, he began to bring up the rear. Without any objection from Dorado he mounted a mare on three successive days, although the mounts we saw were inadequate. The mare had a yearling foal. We did not see the end of the story, but it seemed that Dorado, feeling his strength fail, was content to let his beloved heir take over the band.

We saw a second example of complete band takeover without physical conflict when Careto (Blaze) was dying of tetanus. Although the claimant was a stallion rather than a bachelor, it gives an insight into how a bachelor can inherit a band from a sick stallion.

Little Careto always lived in the middle of others, even covering his mares without separating the band. But when we arrived in 2010 he was not there. After three days of searching we found his band grazing kilometres away from the others. He was standing apart, not watching nor resting but somehow withdrawn. A pickup passed along the track. The mares startled and ran, but round in circles near him, not leaving him.

He was very lame of a hind foot. The next day he was worse, and moved with difficulty. The

*Fig. 6.19  Dorado (centre), beside his favourite mole Vaso de Leche. At the left, the mole that died of pitium infection not long after.*

*Fig. 6.20    Careto, who always lived in the middle of the Camaruco herd, covers a mare regardless of his neighbours. The big black horse watching us is Furia; the group on the right are bachelors.*

third day he was hunched up, obviously in agony, his hind legs splayed apart like a dog trying to defecate. He did not seem to be able to eat, although all the rest were grazing. A large group was a kilometre away. Suddenly the mares, all together, marched purposefully towards it, with Careto hobbling after them as best he could.

We took some time making a detour round the action, arriving to see Jotero herding the band into his own, galloping round the mixed troupe in circles while Humo, Guapo and a pair of other stallions watched without interfering. When Careto finally arrived he stood by them and, when Jotero came round, faced him, stamped and squealed. Jotero took no notice but galloped by. He was having trouble with a cream mare who wanted to get back to Careto, who repeated his 'stop there!' signal again and again, to no avail: Jotero simply ignored him, continuing his herding and circling. After some ten minutes of repeating his signals and being ignored, Careto resigned. He turned and hobbled away in a straight line over the savannah without a backward glance.

Ramón, who looked to be Careto's son and was a novice stallion, left his two mares and ran after him, reaching out to touch Careto's face. But Careto shook his head without greeting him or stopping and hobbled on. Ramón returned slowly to his mares.

Careto found a puddle and tried to drink, but could not. He continued in his straight line into some acacia. The *vaqueros* saw him there next day, but he was dead the day after.

Meanwhile Jotero had a band of over thirty head, and drove himself desperately to keep them together. But Careto's mares did not like his constant harassment and left over the next few days until only his original band remained.

What is striking about this incident is the behaviour of the mares. When Careto was merely lame they were loyal to him, but when he was obviously incapacitated they abandoned him and went to other company. Jotero, too, recognized his incapacity to follow up his threats. And when Careto realized he was invalid in the eyes of all, he went off to die alone.

Perhaps this is what happens in the winter when a stallion sickens. When he is too ill to be effective the mares leave him, and the bachelors are often not far away.

## What Makes a Successful Stallion?

A large number of viable foals, or in the case of the cimarrons, yearlings, for foal mortality is high. Here, home range quality, which might affect other populations, is meaningless. What makes a stallion successful depends on his attractiveness in the eyes of the mares. Three factors emerge: how long he lives, how many mares he covers, and how many foals live to be a year old.

Bachelors acquired their first mares when they were about seven years old, and continued breeding for the rest of their lives. In other populations old stallions lose their mares to bachelors. In the *llanos* they did not. In fact, the older a stallion, the more mares were with him. In the last year we saw Bambú (2008) he was fairly crippled by arthritis: he could barely canter, and that only stiffly. He would have been no match for a strong eight-year-old in a fight. But no bachelor ever challenged him. Eight mares were with him. Humo, in the year before he disappeared, showed no signs of age but had nine mares; Careto had eight when he died aged about seventeen, again showing no signs of age (so Bambú was probably much older). Stallions went on accumulating mares, and inspiring more loyalty from them, the older they were: these bands were the most stable we saw. The simple virtue of surviving for a long time seemed to increase a stallion's attractiveness in the eyes of the mares: good genes for the foal.

Many mares did not appear regularly in any band, but every stallion had his core of faithful ones. Novice stallions often lost their mares, turning up with others the next year. But as the years passed, the core members of the bands became more stable, and stallions often had favourite mares. Surprisingly, their choice did not seem to depend on fecundity or condition. Guapo's favourite, from whom he never parted, was a thin cream mare who never produced a foal in four years. Eventually she died a walking skeleton. Nicolás, in 2011, tended an equally decrepit grey mare who eventually died. On marches to water she could not keep up, so he stayed behind with her. In a cattle round-up stampede he even ran back and stayed with her while the *llaneros* galloped past. The ability to produce foals did not seem to affect a stallion's choice of favourite.

In other populations, stallions defend their mares as much as possible, though they cannot prevent a mare from leaving if she is determined to change bands. The cimarron stallions only protected their mating rights, defending mares against the advances of other males only when they were in season. Jotero, though, adopted the strategy of having as many mares as possible. Although his band lived with the main mass it was almost invariably at one extreme of it, and he herded them often: a *jota* is a traditional dance in which the men whirl around the women.

*Different stallion strategies*

Although he was concerned for his mares, Jotero never took any notice of his foals. He was also the only stallion we saw leading his band in flight: all the others always brought up the rear. We wondered whether he was nobly leading them away from danger or simply legging it faster.

Amiguete had a completely different strategy. He often wandered off, leaving his mares at times when many bands were together. Students who believed in photographic evidence for identifying which mares were in whose band often showed me photos of Amiguete standing proudly in front of Humo's mares, Furia's mares, Guapo's mares or any others. Amiguete maintained such good relations with all the other stallions that they did not object to his posing with their mares. However, one year I counted seven sabino foals outside his band, born to non-sabino mares. It is a dominant colour, there were no other sabino stallions and Amiguete's markings were distinctive. His friendly wanderings might not have been as innocent as they seemed.

The second part of Amiguete's strategy was foal protection. He tended his foals, retrieving them when they strayed and standing over them when they slept, as their mothers do. He even stood guard over sleeping mares, too. Like Bambú (who was probably his father, judging from build and the broadness of the blaze; they had a close relationship), he often played gently with small foals. Once, in a cattle round-up when all the herd was in full stampede with the *llaneros* galloping after them, a small foal got left behind. Without others beside them, foals stop running. Amiguete whirled out of the stampede at full gallop, charged towards the line of five *llaneros* bearing down on the foal, retrieved him and headed back towards the fast-disappearing herd, nudging the foal along with his nose. Even the *llaneros* were so full of admiration that they slackened speed.

Amiguete was not the only stallion who regularly retrieved foals from straying. During the first week or so of a foal's life their mothers are most attentive to them and do not let them out of sight; later, they do not bother so much. If anyone retrieves a laggard foal it is the stallion. In the *llanos* small rescues happened almost every day. If a foal was sleeping and the band, including the mother, drifted on, the stallion would go back for the foal. Once the whole herd was filing along a narrow path through the bushes, a seemingly endless column, with band after band followed by its stallion. Suddenly Elegante turned, ran back a hundred metres, nudged out a foal and hustled him back up the column to his mother, who did not even seem to have noticed he was missing.

Apart from retrieving foals, stallions also spend time interacting with them. Small foals seem particularly attracted to their fathers, and approach them jaw-clapping. The stallion often leans his neck into the foal's open jaws. As a colt foal grows, this turns into a very gentle game of neck-wrestling. By the age of three months colt foals usually spend more time being and playing with their fathers than their mothers. As they mature, the stallion carefully raises the standards of play until, at two years old, they are able to play in the hectic fashion normal in the bachelor band they will join.

*Fig. 6.21    A Cotopaxi stallion herds a straying foal back to its mother. (Photo: Javier Solis)*

Fig. 6.22    *Colt foals are particularly attracted to their fathers (here, Bambú), who play gently with them.*

On the *páramo* of Cotopaxi, where numerous bands often grazed close together, one year there were twenty-five bachelors in three fluctuating bands: the maxi-bachelors, apparently around five to seven years old, strong and boisterous; the middles, somewhat younger; and the mini-bachelors, two- and three-year-olds. Whenever one of these bands approached a natal band the stallion came out to investigate. With the maxis he played, roughly; with the middles, less roughly; with the minis, his contacts were careful and gentle as he examined each one methodically. He would then let a yearling son contact and play with the minis, but would drive him back to the band if he tried to approach the maxis. We saw the same behaviour in seven different stallions, each on various occasions.

### Paternal investment in foals

This paternal care of foals and education of sons gets little consideration in the scientific literature, though Berger, Feist, Boyd and Tyler all mention paternal behaviour, in particular foal retrieval in feral horses. It is particularly visible in the cimarrons but the pottoka stallions behave the same, and so do domestic stallions who are lucky enough to live with their foals. When predators are around, a strong paternal interest in foals adds to stallion success: Amiguete's strategy, though not Jotero's.

Juan Carranza, a deer ethologist, was struck by my tales of stallions' care for foals, since such behaviour is unknown in deer. Then he asked a curious question: 'Why do mares come in season only nine days after giving birth?'

'Because they have an eleven-month gestation', I said, stupidly missing the point. 'If they don't get pregnant in foal heat, they come in again three weeks later.'

'But why eleven months?' he asked. 'They're not so big that it's necessary. Cattle only go nine months, deer seven. Could it be because it is important for the foal's survival to have the stallion close by and interested when it is small?'

In another of those wonderful eureka moments a number of observed facts suddenly became linked into a larger pattern. Foals need to suckle more often than ruminants' calves, so mares do not cache their young and wander off as many ruminants do. Foals need to be close to their mothers, but having a small foal at foot presupposes a responsibility that a mare has difficulty completing, for eating enough to feed a growing foal takes almost all of her time and attention. Small foals are vulnerable and need protection.

Mares are extremely attentive to their foals' straying during the first week of life, often trotting anxiously after them or calling them back with soft nickers. After their foal heat, though, they are more careless and often drift away grazing while foals are sleeping. Unless the foal leaps to his feet and starts trying to locate her, or calling, the mare usually seems not to have noticed his absence. I had put this down to the mare's growing need for food and the growing reliability of the foal's bond to his mother, but perhaps the grand scheme of things counts on paternal protection.

The natal band allows for paternal investment of attention in protection for small foals, for permanent association means the stallion is (almost) certain which are his. Is that the reason why horses universally adopt this mating/social arrangement? Berger's mustangs often raped mares after band takeovers, causing abortion in the early months of pregnancy. These mares did not produce more foals as a result, for they do not necessarily come into season soon, and foals born late in the year have a lower chance of survival anyway. It does, however, mean that the stallions avoid investing protection in foals that are definitely not theirs.

The paternal protection hypothesis needs more rigorous investigation, but a number of pointers indicate that investigation is worthwhile.

Firstly, in Galicia some areas are heavily wolf-infested and others not, but all the free-living ponies have the normal 1:25 or so stallion/mare ratio. In wolf-free areas natal bands comprise around five mares, the remaining mares living in small stallion-free groups as is usual under this management. In wolf-infested zones all mares live in natal bands, which as consequence are very much bigger (Barciela Garcia). The mares know where protection lies, even if it means living in an uncomfortably large band. Laura Lagos saw that mares abandoned a stallion who failed to thrive on the mountain, and went to others.[31]

Similarly Stevens (1990) saw that, on an island, mares in single stallion bands were more likely to change bands than ones in two-stallion bands. Now that many US feral mares receive contraception to prevent excessive breeding rates, there are abundant figures to show that mares with foals seldom change bands whereas ones without, for natural or treatment reasons, are much more likely to do so (Nuñez et al. 2009).

Secondly, a village in Leon has, collectively, some hundred or so mares breeding foals for meat in high mountain country. There are four stallions. A friend with twenty-six mature mares and one stallion usually had about twenty-four foals every year. When wolf hunting was banned and the wolf population grew enormously, his yearly crop dropped to an average of seven, all from the mares who stayed with the stallion. Others in the village said the same. By increasing the number of stallions the foal crop recovered. Stallions are effective foal-protectors.

Thirdly, foal retrieval is much more obvious in our cimarrons, where puma predation is a very real possibility, than in the pottokas or the equally predation-free Cotopaxi horses. But this is where we need a decent long-term study comparing two populations of the same blood living in the same conditions except for predator danger. In the cimarrons, predation would favour stallions with greater protective behaviour.

Fourthly, studies on wolf predation on foals in Galicia showed that after seven months they were more or less invulnerable to wolves (Lagos 2013). In the winter, when foals are big, stallions are less attentive to the cohesion of their bands. On the infrequent occasions that mares with foals change bands they generally do so in the winter.

Finally, numerous experiences with both domestic and feral horses have shown me that stallions are more excited by the sight of a mare with a small foal than a mare alone. I had thought that the foal showed the stallion that the mare was a breeding proposition, but perhaps the sight of an unprotected foal is what excites his interest.

Perhaps this also gives an answer to the Patagonia baguales' foal loss to puma: the stallions, separated by only a few generations from domestic pasture-breeding stock heavily selected for docile, non-protective behaviour, have not had enough time for paternal protection to be re-selected. In contrast Hodei, the black pottoka stallion, rapidly understood the danger posed by an electric fence newly erected to prevent them harassing feeding goats. When the band first approached it, a mare touched it, whirled round, and all fled. They re-approached, a different mare touched it, and all fled again. The third time they approached, Hodei ran up from behind and herded them away furiously; he never let them near white tape again, to the goatherd's admiration.

These observations convince me that we should look more closely at paternal protection as a factor in foal survival especially where predators are present: the conditions under which horses evolved.

*Strategy and character*

Stallion success in the *llanos*, then, depends on three factors: living a long and healthy life, protecting his mating rights over as many mares as possible, and protecting and educating his foals. With regard to the last two, Jotero's strategy concentrated on accumulating mares and Amiguete's on ensuring his confirmed foals survived (though the ones resulting from sneak-mating were rather left to chance). Most stallions do a bit of both. Their relative success does not depend on overt competition – in other populations, conflictive stallions have been shown to have less breeding success than ones who avoid conflict – but on being capable of attracting mares and ensuring their foals survive.

The pottoka stallions, too, show differences in character or strategy that contribute to their relative success. Hodei, the black stallion, was a deeply serious little horse who managed a band of up to thirteen with great responsibility. When hunters left open the gate that leads to high mountains the band roamed and I could not find them. But when the weather turned bad they were at the gate clamouring to get in. I opened it and Hodei pushed past them, threatening them in herding posture until they stood still. He ran down the hill alert for danger. Seeing none, he let them move some couple of hundred metres – bucking and cavorting with glee to be back – stopped them again and scouted ahead. He repeated this four times before letting them down to the shelter of the woods. Hodei's mares were totally loyal to him.

Gabiri the piebald is more like Amiguete, careless about his mares, who stray about especially in winter, but he interacts more with his foals than Hodei. He is also the only stallion who leads his band on the march.

Ibai, who may be Hodei's son, was only two when he eloped with two-year-old Txori, and by four had attracted three more mares. He took his responsibilities seriously despite his extreme youth, and has never looked for trouble with other stallions. But Pintxo, at four, was a frivolous lad, associating for a few days at a time with any wandering mare but abandoning her again to play with his buddies. Nevertheless when a huge Percheron stallion invaded the farm he fought savagely and defeated him. Larrun and her daughters were with him at the time; otherwise, I suspect, he would have played with the giant as he did with other domestic stallions whenever he escaped. When he became a full stallion on Hodei's death, he flew aggressively towards any other stallion, but after a couple of years he calmed down.

Ibai was brought up by Hodei; Pintxo in a field with two domestic horses. How much of their differences are down to character or strategy and how much to their role models?

*New home ranges*

The pottokas have home ranges; all interact at a favourite high col, el Risquillo. Hodei's band stayed on the heights, and no other bands were ever seen there; after his death, his son Ekain took the range. Pintxo's home range is a little lower down. Gabiri and Ibai interchange the Serrana home range and the woods (and some mares). The disproportionate preponderance of juveniles in this fast-growing population gives an insight into home range selection for a bachelor. There is no shortage of food, but the existing home ranges take up most of the area. There are many gates, which people continually leave open. Only rarely does a natal band get out, but the bachelors are determined escapers, exploring the surrounding wooded mountains for kilometres around. Pintxo, when beginning to take a serious interest in mares, started returning unless he had a mare with him. Ibai, on eloping with Txori, escaped immediately, though he had never done so before. Even the cimarron novice stallions still go away from the main herd. Bachelors are scouting for new home ranges to which they will take their mares when they acquire them, rather than, as popular legend has it, being thrown out by their fathers. Renée Meissner, who studies the Przewalski herd released in Mongolia, has reached the same conclusion.

## Two-Stallion Bands

The population in which I have seen most two-stallion bands is on Cotopaxi, where nine out of twenty-four natal bands had two stallions; on the other hand there were no Moles in natal bands. Many bands grazed together in two areas around water. While some bands always maintained a thirty-metre no-man's land between them and the next, some grazed alongside and some actually mingled together as the Camaruco cimarrons do. All the bands that repeatedly fused, whether during a few minutes, hours or days, had two stallions. This added weight

*Fig. 6.23   Nicordón (left) and Nicolás (centre) maintain their shared band with equal, cooperative relations. Behind and to the right of Nicolás is Amiguete, rather fat, whose band is thoroughly fused with the Nicos'. There may be another natal band here too.*

to my suspicions that only socially confident stallions allow their bands to intermingle with others, for in the *llanos* young or sick stallions, or ones with a mare in season, stayed separate from the main mass. When a novice stallion like little Ramón realized that a mature one like Humo would respect his signals, he re-entered the mass.

In the Camoruco cimarrons two stallions in a band were either fellow-travellers, weak stallions with one mare each who lived together, or friends who shared mares, but in the Cotopaxi bands we examined in detail, the two stallions usually had different roles. One stayed with the mares, marginalizing the other who, as a result, made the inter-band contacts. This marginalization was so subtle as to be barely noticeable; indeed the two stallions could often be seen grazing so close together they seemed to be shadows, without any friction. Yet one was always between the other and the mares, or one particular mare. Their consciousness of each other's precise location was constant and impressive – except when the mare-guarder happily lay flat to sleep while the other took look-out duty.

In one band, the external stallion (NegB) went off to check around when they moved to a new grazing zone, but when he returned the mares´ stallion, Brillante, dashed out some seventy metres, displayed furiously and they fought, seriously but briefly, before ritual dunging. Neither seemed to have won. They then strolled back to the band side by side, perfectly relaxed. Checking the bachelors before allowing his son to contact them fell to Brillante, but when he played with a rough maxi-bachelor and squealed on being bitten, NegB charged the bachelor and drove him away. NegB also retrieved Brillante's son when he got left behind. In other words, the relationship was not the clear dominance/submission one often proposed, but was considerably more complex: neither Linklater's uneasy temporary truce nor Feh's cooperative alliance, but an amalgam of the two. In other two-stallion bands the proportion

*Fig. 6.24   Two-stallion band on Cotopaxi showing shared duties. Here NegB is on duty while Brillante rests; in Fig. 5.3, their roles are reversed. (Photo: Javier Solis)*

of the two elements in the amalgam differed, from constant exasperated marginalization to invariably friendly sharing of duties. Having seen different populations and individuals vary so enormously in male-male friendliness or rivalry, I suspect that we can arrive at no fixed formula without knowing a great deal more about the variables. We do not have a way of assessing character in feral stallions, although the mares certainly do.

## Social Relations within a Band

In most feral populations the breeding season is the time when bands are most stable and few band changes take place. In the cimarrons, bands fluctuated more.

*Band identity*
Feral mares usually eject non-members from their bands (as do domestic horse groups), even when the stallion welcomes them. A filly in natal dispersal, ejected from her natal band by her father when she first comes in season, may be attracted by the smell of a stallion in another band and approach it (if the bachelors don't find her first). The stallion drives her in, the mares drive her out, and she spends a couple of stressful weeks dithering on the outskirts of the band until the mares gradually accept her. Her acceptance may be due to her acquisition of the band's common smell: bands with clear home ranges all roll in selected spots, the stallion often rolling both first and last. The striking, up-wind position of the Camoruco stallion in the post-stampede *piña*, when his scent bathes the members of his band, also suggests that his individual smell is important to band identity.

We never saw the permanent mares of a Camoruco band eject floaters (except when forming post-stampede *piñas*), but stallions did. On many occasions we saw a stallion chase a mare out of his band and, when another stallion appeared at a gallop, hand her over to him as if to say: 'She's yours, so why don't you keep a better eye on her?' Sometimes the stallions made a brief, friendly contact before the second drove the mare away. Once on Cotopaxi a mare and her foal, who had gone up a bank without realizing the others were not following, dashed down again into the wrong band and were summarily chased out by the stallion, to be retrieved in this way by her own stallion. Significantly, a stallion chasing a mare away does not use the herding posture: he reserves that for members of his own band. Herding is, then, not an aggressive move, although he is driving them, but one used to protect them.[32]

*Bonds between individuals*
These fall into two categories: kinship bonds and friendship bonds. They are expressed by affiliative behaviour: the two individuals are found together more often than with any other horse and they make affectionate physical contact. They touch and smell noses (even when they know perfectly well who the other is), touch and nibble the face, neck or shoulder of the other; one passes their head or neck over the other's, or lays their head and neck across the other's back; on seeing something interesting one touches the other's shoulder; they stand head to tail using the swish of each other's tail to keep the face fly-free. They share individual space.

The concept of individual space is an important one, shared by many social animals including us. Horses regard the space around them, a little more than a metre around their bodies, as their own, and resent the intrusion of another unless it be family or friend. Even then the

Fig. 6.25   *Affiliative closeness shown by three pottoka bachelors. Oihan, centre, seems to resent the intrusion of Pintxo, right, in his shared moment with Eder.*

Fig. 6.26   *As well as a means of identifying individuals, smell seems important in the maintenance of bonds.*

intruder adopts specific body attitudes that signify friendly intentions rather than mere careless intrusion: for instance the approach before mutual grooming is slow and slouchy, the approach inviting play is bouncy, the approach before a friendly greeting is ears-forward and free of tension.

Normally, when grazing or on the march, horses respect each other's space, though when resting, respect for space may be relaxed. The pottoka bands often rest in a huddle in the shade; the cimarrons did not, but stood in lines facing the breeze with a space between them. Their post-stampede *piñas* were structured huddles that illustrate the role of huddling in bonding, also shown by the pottokas' way of shoving rather than aggressing when in competition for focal goodies.

A form of contact that has received no attention is olfactory contact. Resting close together, one horse's nose is usually a hand's breadth from its neighbour's shoulder or belly. Watching carefully, you see that from time to time the nostrils flare as the horse fills them with the scent of his neighbour. Such contact is also important in the *piña*. We have such a poor sense of smell that its importance to horses, especially in forming bonds, has not been investigated.

### Maternal-filial bond

During the first week of a foal's life the maintenance of the bond is mostly based on the mother's behaviour, but as the foal grows he gradually takes the greater share of the relationship. When the foal suckles, his mother turns to smell and touch his rump (a handy moment for a would-be foal tamer to touch and scratch his rump too). Cameron saw that when foals are startled they run to their mothers and suckle, but often for only a few seconds, not long

*Fig. 6.27   Early maternal behaviour. Gazte, rather annoyed, tries to keep an eye on her day-old colt Eder. Left, his father Gabiri.*

enough to extract milk. Our figures on suckling times show two clear peaks, one around 3–5 seconds and the other at 55–65 seconds, the second being a feeding bout. 'Non-nutritional suckling' seems to calm and reassure the foal, perhaps helped by the smell of a secretion on the udder. In domestic weaning, stressed youngsters are apt to search for any protuberance to suckle, a common origin of crib-biting.

A young foal only plays alone, running around his mother, but as he grows he forms friendships through contacting, playing and mutual grooming with others. Colts are noticeably more forward than fillies, who do not play-fight but only play synchrony games. By around five months old a foal makes more social contacts with others than with his mother, who is simply the milk-bar.

Weaning normally takes place some two to three months before the birth of the next foal: for cimarrons at around eighteen months, but in more fecund populations like the pottokas, at eight or nine months. Often the mare drops the hip nearest to the foal as he tries to suckle, effectively barring access to the udder, or raises the hind leg in warning. However, the affective bond is not broken abruptly, as is often the case in domestic horses. The youngster gradually spends more time away from his mother, being actively driven away if he tries to share feeding time with his younger sibling. He forms friendship bonds with other youngsters in play, but follows his mother on the march and runs to her when frightened. Colt foals, because of their propensity to play, are generally more independent at a year or fifteen months than fillies.

Feral mares mutually groom with their foals, especially yearlings, and with the stallion, but not with each other.

Maternal-filial bonds are finally broken at natal dispersal. Some fillies are so attached to their mothers that they return to them after being covered by a non-band male. These fillies do not make good mothers, for they are so dependent on their own mothers that they neglect their foals (Monard *et al.* 1996b). On the other hand, a filly who bonds well into her new band is a more successful mother than one who does not, so that the dependency on bonds has to strike a delicate balance.

In the pottokas, we have seen two instances of over-strong maternal-filial bonds. The mare Indar ('Strength') foaled at only two years of age and did not foal the next year. She was particularly attached to her filly Euri, so much so that when Euri, at two years old, left her natal band, Indar went with her. Euri went to Gabiri's band, but since Indar had been born into this band, Gabiri would not accept her back. Euri spent uncomfortable months looking for a solution, with Indar trailing after her. Finally Euri took up with young Pintxo, then Ibai, and after a couple of months Indar left her and went back to Hodei for the birth of her new foal.

Argi (Light) was so firmly attached to her mother Larrun that she refused to leave her natal band; Gabiri, her father, equally refused to cover her. Finally both went to join Pintxo and, later, Ibai. Argi did not foal until she was five.

These examples show that forming over-strong bonds can be as problematical as not forming strong enough bonds.

*Paternal bonds* (see *above*)

Apart from retrieving and protecting their foals and choosing whether to let them interact with those of other bands, stallions groom and play with them, especially their sons. Colts are particularly attracted by their fathers and at three months often spend more time with them than with their mothers. Stallions sometimes play with passing bachelors who may be their sons, as Berger saw, so these father-son bonds are longer-lasting than mother-son bonds.

Contrary to popular belief, stallions do not see their sons as competition. Like other investigators, I have not seen a stallion forcibly eject a son from the band. The natal dispersal of colts seems to be voluntary. What I have seen several times in the pottokas is a stallion aggressively ejecting a colt who was not his son but brought to the band as a foal by his dam. In these cases the stallion tolerated the colt well until he showed sexual interest – in two cases, performing Flehmen on smelling an in-season mare's urine – a sign that it was time for him to leave the band.

Pintxo had a son Bihurri, of whom he was particularly fond. When the mare Hiru came in season, Bihurri repeatedly tried to mate her, over several days, while Pintxo watched unconcerned. When Pintxo mounted her, Bihurri ran to her and courted her frantically, effectively helping his father by blocking her from moving forward. So much for fathers seeing their sons as competition.

### Sibling bonds
Strong bonds form between older and younger siblings, especially females, who often groom together both in the cimarrons and the pottokas. One orphan yearling cimarron was so attached to his three-year-old sister than he appeared to be her son.

*Fig. 6.28   Bihurri, a two-year-old colt, mounts a rather unwilling Hiru while his father Pintxo, immediately behind, takes no notice.*

*Fig. 6.29    Natal band stallion playing with a passing bachelor. (Photo: Javier Solis)*

## Friendship bonds

These are particularly strong and lasting between males. Lucky colt foals have one or two more colts to play with; cimarron colts have no difficulty in finding playmates since the bands so frequently merge. Colts, since their main play mode is play-fighting, soon become too rough for fillies and are aggressively rejected; if alone in the band they play with their fathers. When older colts play with younger ones, they are noticeably gentler than when playing together.

However we have seen, on several occasions, that when a two-year-old colt comes out from his natal band and approaches a passing band of Latin Kings, these play roughly with him as if testing to see whether he is ready to join them.

Male friendship bonds even survive a filly joining the bachelor band. Mature cimarron stallions also greet and occasionally play with each other; we are not certain if they were in the same bachelor band together.

Stallions may have favourite mares. If temporary, this is usually an indication that the mare will soon come in season, but some of these love affairs last years.

Mares, on the other hand, do not show strong evidence of friendship apart from being in the same band, though detailed analysis of their movements shows that they may indeed prefer to associate with one partner more than another. Feral mares do not groom each other; nor do they become inseparable. When a stallion dies the mares may split up and join different bands, or may stay together. The excessive bonding sometimes seen in domestic horses does not appear to be natural, but a pathological response to insecurity and anxiety.

*Mare-stallion bond*

Mares choose to be with a particular stallion, and loyal mares are better breeders than ones who change bands. Since the stallion usually stays with and follows the mares, their bond to him is seldom obvious. The emphasis of interpretation has been on male 'possession' rather than on female choice. However, in populations where bands fuse freely the importance of female choice is clear. When Careto was lame, his startled mares ran off but round in circles, waiting for him. Similarly, in the fused bands on Cotopaxi, some mares fled with their stallion while the others stayed with theirs. Mares know where their protection lies.

## A STUDY ON SOCIAL INTERACTION ... TRANSLATED

Two students, Enrique Zunzunegui and Mariana Puchet, made a small but admirably detailed study of all the social interactions within two bands during two weeks. One band (Opaco) had one stallion, five mares and three foals; the other (the Nicos) two stallions, four mares, one foal and three young colts one to two years old. The students scored thirty-eight behavioural measures. Their results gave numerical backing to what we had seen. In both bands, 67% of the total interactions observed involved the stallion, and 80% of all interactions were affiliative, 20% agonistic. But these bald figures, typical of the summaries in ethological studies, overlook the rich stories that hide behind the lines of ticks in columns.

Opaco has a mare coming into season, but not yet fully willing. He makes hopeful sexual approaches and touches (score affiliative/sexual) but she rejects him (score agonistic). He herds the mares together often. He also makes mistakes about who is in season. Stallions often do this: with the ground liberally sprinkled with the scent of a willing mare, a stallion is

*Fig. 6.30  Affiliative contact, stallion and mare. (Photo: Javier Solis)*

*Fig. 6.31    A mare refuses a stallion's attentions when she is not in season. Stallions smell the pheromone in an in-season mare's urine, but often mistake which mare left it. (Photo: Javier Solis)*

liable to sniff it, show Flehmen repeatedly and rush up to the nearest mare who catches his eye, only to be firmly rebuffed. In Opaco's case the right mare accepts him a couple of days later, although his mounts are often inadequate. She has a small foal, so may not be ovulating.

His own aggressions are limited to strangers: he chases off the stallion in the neighbouring band, also a mule (it is 2011). The mare attacks the mule, too. Also, after smelling him carefully, Opaco head-thrusts at a youngster who does not belong to his band.

There are no other aggressions within the band, but many friendly contacts between the mares, who rest together in parallel, not quite touching. They do not have particular friends; nor do they mutually groom. One has no contact with anybody at all, not even Opaco, who regularly greets all the other mares and the foals. We see the contacts between two young foals grow: one is particularly bold in his approaches to the other, to Opaco and, at one point, to an egret. The third foal, who is younger, makes contact only with his mother.

In the Nicos' band, mares groom with their yearlings, the two stallions groom each other, and Nicolás grooms with his beloved thin mare, the one he went back to accompany when she could not keep up with a stampede. Here the aggressions arise because Nicordón does not like this mare, but kicks her if she comes close. Also, there is a mare coming into season who accepts Nicordón's courtship, but not that of Nicolás. Nevertheless there are no hard feelings between the two stallions, who may be brothers.

These results correlate with other studies. Stallions make the majority of the social contacts, and with all members of the band. Mares, in contrast, have few social contacts except with their offspring, though they do rest side by side as if finding peace in each other's shade. Even when they have weaned a foal because another is on the way, or indeed born, they maintain contacts with their yearlings. There is very little aggression in such a band, but ample evidence for peaceful coexistence.

### What triggers aggression?

When we looked at the proximal causes for aggressions within a band (what triggers them off), which we recorded in the *llanos* every year, we counted the following as agonistic: ears back, head-thrust, bite, charge, one-leg kick that misses, two-leg kick that usually connects, foreleg stamp and squeal. These last two are usually given only by stallions to other males, or by mares rejecting courtship.

52 per cent mare rejecting a stallion's sexual advances when she is not in season;
13 per cent in-season mare to bachelor or in-band colt;
4 per cent mare towards yearling or two-year-old who has come too close;
3 per cent mare to other mare, cause unknown;
5 per cent to weaned youngster trying to suckle with sibling;
3 per cent mare to stallion grazing gradually too close;
2 per cent mare protecting very young foal from playing youngsters;
1 per cent rejecting advance of other's small foal;
remainder to donkeys, mules or cows.

*Fig. 6.32   Pottoka mare with a new-born foal aggresses her weaned yearling, who was trying to nurse.*

*Fig. 6.33    Yearling filly Serrana aggresses three-year-old bachelor Pintxo, who was playing too roughly with her.*

*Fig. 6.34    Mare-foal aggression during nursing. (Photo: Javier Solis)*

The same causes are shown by the pottokas, where we have also seen: foals several months old aggress and successfully drive away stallions sexually interested (mistakenly) in the foals` mothers; mares aggressing a filly in natal dispersal who has just joined the band; filly foals aggressing colt foals who start play-fighting with them; mild annoyance (ears-back) from a stallion to an in-season daughter attracted by his smell; stallions chasing out their daughters from the band. Mares have been seen to aggress stallions who appear sexually interested in the mares' yearling daughters, but only when both mare and daughter have recently joined the band so that the normal inbreeding prohibition does not hold.

Stallions are very rarely aggressive to band members, even cheeky youngsters, except when ejecting daughters or non-son colts. Other studies seldom classify or give the proportions of proximal causes for aggressions, but the following have been examined in studies on particular behaviours, for instance nursing and natal dispersal.

- Maternal aggression during nursing, starting when the foal is around three weeks old. The mare is suckling as normal but suddenly turns and bites the foal furiously, or kicks him. She then behaves as if nothing has happened and allows the foal to resume suckling.
  Foals are born without teeth, which they cut at this time. Until the teeth meet and wear flat, they are sharp. If they touch the udder …
- During mutual grooming. Equally sudden aggressions can take place.
- During colts' play, suddenly, terminating the game.
  (All the above seem to be objections to over-enthusiastic use of teeth.)
- A higher rate of aggression towards two-year-olds than towards yearlings: perhaps a suggestion it is time for them to leave the band and find another. Nevertheless, the proximal cause for a filly's dispersal is not aggression, but coming into season (Monard *et al.* 1996a).

Almost all these aggressions are low-intensity: ears back, head-thrust or the one-leg kick that does not connect but merely warns the other to keep a distance.

Notably we do not see, either in the literature or in my observations, in-band aggression caused by resource competition. They shove.

The response to aggression is to move away. We can see that the proximal or trigger causes fall into four groups: ones about not wanting sex, ones about teeth, ones about avoiding inbreeding, and ones that mark stages in a youngster's life-history. The overall effect, though, is to make horses very aware that others have a space around them that can only be entered to make friendly contacts or to mate, both of which carry specific signals: careless invasions are angrily repelled. 'Respect my space' is the key to peaceful coexistence, the final cause of in-band aggressions.

This message cannot be taught by a mare to her foal, at least until the foal is weaned. The other mares in the band, though, can and do teach others' foals and the weaned youngsters to be careful around them, leaving always that respectful distance. As they grow, youngsters become aware that they, too, have an individual space and the right to repel intruders from it.

Why is this so important?

In a stampede, respect for space keeps them from colliding. Their survival depends on it. The distance they maintain, a little over a metre, is the same as the space into which intrusion provokes aggression during daily life. When afraid, either of external threats like puma or in-band ones from angry mares, horses do not enter each other's space.

## SOCIAL ORGANIZATION: A SUMMARY

We are now in a position to draw together the conclusions from previous chapters and summarize the 'whys' and 'hows' of horses' social lives.

Horses took to social living in the Miocene, when predators also triggered a series of physical adaptations to facilitate detection and mass flight. The natal band is a self-organizing cooperative defence unit composed of several mares, offspring, and one or two stallions whose heightened reactions to threat provide the band's early-warning system and initiate synchronized mass escape.

The most vulnerable members of the band are small foals. Stallions take the major responsibility for their safety and cohesion while mares are responsible for their healthy growth. Mares choose stallions for reasons that may vary with environmental conditions. Though they can, and do, change stallions, loyal mares breed better. Stable, peaceful bands whose stallions avoid conflict also breed better, and both stallions and mares defend band stability.

The stallion's compensation for his protection is his exclusive right to breed with the band's mares, a right he defends. Both stallions and mares avoid investment in foals who are not theirs, the basis of the universal polygynous female-defence mating system. However, the social system might more accurately be called one of foal defence.

Within bands there is no aggressive competition for maintenance resources. The great majority of social interactions are affiliative, weaving a network of bonds based on kinship and friendship. Aggression is rare and limited to specific proximal causes including incest avoidance, rejection of inappropriate courtship, life stages and use of teeth. Aggression provokes avoidance. Its final cause is the establishment and maintenance of the concept of individual space, vital during mass flight to avoid collisions.

Bachelors live in bands that provide ample opportunities for exploration, investigation of dangers and future home ranges. In frequent play-fights they determine the relative strength and agility of others in the band and learn to assess rapidly the quality of an unknown opponent, thus minimizing injury in aggressive competition over mares. As they mature, bachelors increasingly practise stallion behaviour patterns like scent marking, vigilance, and herding.

## CHAPTER 7

# 'Horses Have Strict Dominance Hierarchies'

The model of in-band social structure presented here is based on detailed observation of herd behaviour, and especially predator defence behaviour, which conforms to the findings of a new field of research hitherto not applied to horses. The result is a coherent view of horses' social behaviour in terms of adaptation to the ecological niche of a grazing prey animal. Herds or bands stay together and move together through self-organization, without dominants or leaders.

This does not tally with the prevalent view of the social organization of horses. 'Horses have strict dominance hierarchies' is a statement that is widely reproduced or assumed in scientific papers, student textbooks, popular science-based books, tracts on training and on the Internet. The dominance hierarchy model is likely to be the first met by horse-owners wishing to gain knowledge about horses' reactions to each other and to people, and to colour their subsequent interpretation of experiences with them.

This chapter presents arguments to show:

1. That the statement as given by ethologists is widely misinterpreted by non-ethologists.
2. That, on examination, the evidence given to support it is contradictory, confused, and based on unjustified assumptions and parallels.
3. That this evidence may be interpreted in a different light that clarifies the confusion.

As the dominance hierarchy paradigm is so widely accepted and taught, I examine it in detail.

## DEFINING 'DOMINANCE'

First, we must define what 'dominance' and 'dominance hierarchy' mean. In many books and explanations they are not defined, allowing readers to interpret them as they will. The Oxford English Dictionary gives:

*dominance*: 'supreme authority, governing, ruling'.

*authority* is defined as 'the power or right to enforce obedience'.

This is not how ethologists define dominance. To understand why they have changed its definition, a little history is called for.

In 1922 Thorlief Schelderupp-Ebbe watched hens feeding together at a trough and saw that one hen, A, was liable to peck any other; B pecked all the others except A, C pecked all but A and B, and so on down the line to an unfortunate creature that got pecked by all but never pecked back. The idea of a 'peck order' was born. Schelderupp-Ebbe did not claim that hen A was a supreme authority, just that whenever any other hen got in her way when feeding, she pecked it.

The idea of social dominance in the dictionary sense crystallized in the 1930s with Solly Zuckerman's study of a group of captive hamadryas baboons in a large cage in the London Zoo. Zuckerman saw that there was one strong male who had the right to anything he wanted: all the females, the best of the food, the best resting spot and so on. If he had to threaten another to make that individual give up what he wanted, the other deferred to him, cringing and making submissive gestures that simultaneously switched off his aggression and allowed him to have what he wanted. The strong male dominated the group; the others were his subordinates.

Since the α male controlled all the resources, his subordinates curried favour with him by grooming him (seen as appeasement gestures). He was the centre of the group's attention and their leader, and could move them about as he pleased. He could also be a peace-maker: if two subordinates started to squabble, he stopped them. In turn, the subordinates ranked themselves into a hierarchy, giving each other submissive gestures where appropriate and offering to groom higher-ranking members.

The dominant in this case had a particular social role, and the dominance hierarchy reduced outright aggression by reducing it to symbolic threat and submission. The dominant controlled the resources.

Later studies on groups of captive chimpanzees and wolves seemed to show the same picture of an α dominant that gained his position by force and maintained it by threat (Schenkel). He got the best of the resources, had the right to mate with any female he wanted and was the leader. The hierarchy, created by similar relations among others, maintained peace. Konrad Lorenz, ever an influential ethologist (Ch.1), wrote a highly controversial book, *On Aggression*, in which he claimed that the final cause of aggression within groups of animals was to establish a dominance hierarchy in which the most superior animal won the best resources and mates. As he saw it, the dominant was the fittest member of any group in some sense – stronger, more intelligent or with better leadership qualities, and the formation of a hierarchy gave this individual better chances of breeding more like himself. It was, Lorenz thought, a kind of natural selection of the best of the group.

The picture of dominance has a familiar ring. Our history is replete with examples of hierarchical societies in which rulers have undisputed rights to all resources, including in some cases all the women in the kingdom. Rulers direct behaviour and expect submission; royal anger brings bows, scrapes and apologies; but who does not want to be the royal favourite? Unwanted gifts are showered on kings in the hope of winning favours. Royal blood was thought to be 'better' than other blood, too. In our present society status is sought as a valuable asset, signifying power and control over resources, while fame attracts popularity. This early interpretation of dominance hierarchies and their characteristics is almost intuitively clear to us.

However, when studies were made of other social animals, or even of the same species living in natural conditions, the results were not the same. Dominants did not behave in the despotic way they did when none could escape; they had to maintain alliances with their followers too, or others ganged up on them (*Et tu, Brute?*) Subordinates did not give submissive gestures so often, or did not give them at all: they kept out of the dominant's way, or ran off. Females mated with whom they liked, out of the dominant's immediate vicinity if necessary. Dominants did not necessarily have the power to direct others' behaviour, or to lead. Both dominance and submissive gestures were far more obvious in captive animals, and some observers maintained that they were only seen in captivity. Without such an obvious hierarchy as had been seen in the zoo, society ran more harmoniously, a mutual network of give and take. Little by little the original model crumbled. Dominance seemed to have no fixed characteristics, but nevertheless existed.[33] In a notable conference in 1981 each hitherto accepted characteristic of dominance was shown not to exist in some animal society in which dominance-submission relations were claimed (Bernstein 1981, Vessey 1981 and others in the same volume). Some primatologists concluded that hierarchies lay in the eye of the beholder: they were more important to investigators than to the animals (Altman 1981, Rowell 1974).

Yet the very word dominance seems to have the same attraction to the human mind as dominance itself (Adler 1938). Researchers kept using it even when they had violent disagreements as to what it implied. Finally Carlos Drews (1993), in a heroic effort to sort out the warring factions, summarized what everybody had said and gave the only definition that satisfied them all: 'dominance is an attribute of the pattern of repeated, agonistic interactions between two individuals, characterized by a consistent outcome in favour of the same dyad member and a default yielding response of the opponent rather than escalation. The status of the consistent winner is dominant and the loser submissive.'

In other words, if two animals have repeated conflicts, and one always wins while the other always gives up, the first is dominant and the second submissive, or subordinate. All reference to control over resources, authority, control over behaviour, right to expect obedience, leadership, attractiveness or being the focus of the group's attention have been removed. What the conflicts might be about does not matter. No social function for this kind of relationship is implied.

This is the definition now used by ethologists. It does not imply what anyone who speaks Standard English and has not followed this tortured history takes it to mean: that dominance implies authority, supremacy, a quality of character or a particular social role. It simply says that after repeated conflicts between two animals, if one wins without having to fight then that animal is dominant. Hence, ethologists' statements about dominance are widely misinterpreted by the general public.

What the definition does imply is that dominance-submission relations are more than merely winning or losing one contest. They are learned relations that reduce outright aggression to threat and symbolic submission. A subordinate cedes to a dominant without argument.

Although this definition only refers to pairs of animals, if B cedes to A, C to B, and so on, we will find a linear hierarchy A, B, C etc. When there is competition between all for a desired resource, there will be no argument: each will know their place in line and wait their turn. The hierarchy is stable since the relations are consistent, and peace results.

The social, adaptive function of a dominance hierarchy is considered to be reduction of aggression, especially in competition, the situation that most provokes aggressive arguments. Obviously dominants win resource contests, since they win any contest.

The central points of dominance hierarchy theory, then, are stability, reduction of aggression, and consequently resource control by dominants.

## HOW EQUINE 'DOMINANCE' IS MEASURED

Scores of aggression, threat and submission are made whenever two animals come into conflict. Each pair is rated according to dominance-submission relations and the results arranged in a hierarchy.

Most equine researchers agree on basic signs of aggression: ears flat, head-thrust, charge, bite. Whether threat to kick, and kick, are aggressive or defensive is rather more difficult to decide, but dominance researchers include them. Stallions in conflict arch their necks, parallel prance, give foreleg strikes and use the moves seen in play-fighting: rear, squeal, scream, so those go in too. Some, though not all, include a stallion's herding of his mares or foals.

Moving away is taken as a sign of submission. A dominant animal does not necessarily have to threaten a subordinate in order to make it move away: mere approach is often enough. This is called passive displacement. In early studies it was not scored as submission, but now it usually is. Some even favour looking away as a sign of submission (McGreevy 2004).

## Correlations

Having constructed a hierarchy, researchers ask firstly: what makes an animal dominant? Size? Age? Weight? Or some other feature, like length of stay in the group, sex or learning ability? Are dominants superior in some way to others, as Lorenz suggested?

Secondly, they ask: what does rank or status really mean in terms of social life? Are dominants leaders? Do they have better foals? Do stallions prefer dominant mares? Do subordinates start mutual grooming bouts, as they do in primates?

Answers come in the form of correlation coefficients, which measure the chances that two characteristics occur together. Correlation coefficients are difficult to interpret, for they do not necessarily mean there is any functional connection between the two characteristics. For instance, we may ask whether a person's job affects the type of vehicle he drives. We find that, indeed, farmers are more likely to drive all-terrain vehicles and pickups than are office workers.

In this case the relationship is functional, although buying a pickup does not make you a farmer. But if we measure hair length in Europeans below retiring age and make a hierarchy starting with the shortest hair (you can make a hierarchy of any data you want, by arranging the results in a column) we will probably find a reasonable reverse correlation between hair length and strength. We have not proved a kind of reverse Samson effect: rushing out and cutting your hair will not make you stronger. On average, though, European men cut their hair shorter than women and, independently of hairstyle, are stronger. The correlation has no functional significance. It will not even hold true if we measure another group with different hair culture, like Sikhs or Hasidic Jews.

Researchers may overlook this fundamental point when they summarize their conclusions – read the small print.

## The Results

Table 2 summarizes some results of different studies on dominance hierarchies. Some refer to whether a particular feature is present or not (Are there hierarchies? Are they stable?) and others to correlation of rank to another characteristic (age, aggression, leadership).

**Table 2    Some Results of Dominance Studies in Horses**

| Behaviour | | Yes or +ve correlation | | No or -ve correlation |
|---|---|---|---|---|
| Exist within bands | F | Keiper and Sambraus 1986 | F | Feist and McCullough 1976 |
| | F | Rutberg and Greenberg 1990 | F | Berger 1986 |
| | F, D | Houpt and Keiper 1982 | | |
| Hierarchy stable | D | Houpt and Wolski 1980 | F | Keiper and Sambraus 1986 |
| | | | F | Berger 1986 |
| | | | D | van Dierendonck 2005 |
| Age | F | Keiper and Sambraus 1986 | D | Houpt et al. 1978 |
| | M | Tyler 1972 | D | Haag et al. 1980 |
| Size | F | Rutberg and Greenberg 1990 | F | Houpt and Keiper 1982 |
| | M | Tyler 1972 | D | Houpt et al. 1978 |
| | | Houpt and Wolski 1977 | D | Haag et al. 1980 |
| Aggression | M | Heitor et al. 2006 | F | Rutberg & Greenberg 1990 |
| Stallion dominant | F | Feist and McCullough 1976 | F | Houpt and Keiper 1982 |
| Up-hierarchy aggression | D | 19 % Weeks et al. 2000 | M | >5 % Clutton-Brock et al. 1976 |
| | | | M | Wells and von Goldschmidt-Rothschild 1979 |
| Change in mare rank after foaling | M | Stebbins 1974 | F | Keiper and Sambraus 1986 |
| | D | van Dierendonck et al. 2004 | F | Boyd 1980 |
| Foal rank follows dam's rank | D | Houpt and Wolski 1980 | F | Keiper and Sambraus 1986 |
| | D | Araba and Crowell-Davis 1994 | | |
| Mutual grooming near rank | D | Ellard and Crowell-Davis 1989 | F | Kimura 1998 |
| | | | D | van Dierendonck et al. 2004 |
| Mutual grooming start/finish | M | Clutton-Brock et al. 1976 | M | Tyler 1972 |
| Rolling (bachelor band) | F | Feist and McCullough 1976 | M | Stebbins 1974 |
| Leadership | F | Rutberg and Greenberg 1990 | F | Wells and v. Goldschmidt-R 1979 |

F means feral horses,

M free-living horses with management (few stallions, colt culling, winter feed),

D domestic horses.

Why such a wild diversity of results? The answer often given is that researchers use different scoring systems, which is sometimes true.[34] But if rank were such an important social factor, its relevance would emerge despite these differences, give or take a few anomalies. Researchers often do use different scoring systems in studies of the same phenomenon. In studying leadership, Nico, Bourjade, Kreuger, another student Maria Gudiña and I, working independently, all used different data collection systems and different feral populations, but we all came to the same conclusion. There are so many studies that examine rank (I lost count after 200) that some consensus of opinion would be expected. In this case researchers cannot even agree whether dominance hierarchies exist or not.

*Fact:* in a group of horses, some attack, threaten and/or are avoided more than others.

*Question:* what is the social relevance of that fact?

*Accepted answer:* horses have strict dominance hierarchies that act as determining factors in social relations and organization.

*Problem:* rank does not correlate consistently to any feature of social relations.

## What is Wrong?

When we examine the dominance hierarchy paradigm in horses, we find that it rests on a morass of dubious definition, unfounded assumptions, questionable practices and false parallels. Nevertheless, since the paradigm is (almost) universally accepted, the burden of proof rests on me to expose its fallacies and re-interpret the facts in a different, more coherent light.

*Definitions*
Displacing another by aggression, threat or mere presence is taken to signify dominance. I do not argue with Drews' definition, which is crystal clear. But researchers interpret it as meaning that *all* instances of such behaviour contribute to rank, whatever their proximate causes. Aggression is seen in conflict behaviour, but that does not mean that conflict is its only cause, nor that all aggression should contribute to rank assessment. Drews specifies that dominance and submission arise in *repeated* conflicts.

When a mare objects to her foal's biting her teats, is she expressing social dominance? Is the pair in conflict? Or is the mare simply irritated by being bitten? When she defends her newborn foal, or rejects a mistaken suitor, or attacks another horse to win a bucket of food, do these acts really express the same social relations? Should they appear as equivalent anonymous ticks in a little box? Ignoring proximate causes means ignoring the very fabric of social relations that is supposed to be under investigation.

Researchers calculate rank under varying conditions, some highly conflictive and others not. Some really are measuring dominance, some are seeing who wins a one-off fight (which is not repeated conflict), and others are including data on aggression and avoidance that have nothing to do with conflict. Their results will not tally.

Submission is another tricky point. Without submission, dominance cannot exist. But horses have no submissive gestures. All ethologists agree on this point.[35] Therefore, moving away is said to signify submission. However, horses also move away from puma, wolves, motorbikes, flapping plastic, flies, bogs, cold winds and owners trying to catch them, without being thought to be submissive to them. The same reaction cannot be called submission, defence, startle, self-preservation, maintenance and insubordination without creating suspicions of a Humpty-Dumpty use of words to suit the user's purpose. Horses move away from anything they perceive as threatening, whatever it is.

Submission, like dominance, is a highly charged word. Avoidance describes what happens, not what we interpret it to signify.

*Assumptions*

Proximate causes of aggression or threat are assumed to be equivalent. Their final cause is then assumed to be rank maintenance or gain. This is inherent in the scoring system.

Next, rank or status is assumed to be valuable to a horse. 'The advantages of high status are obvious', says McGreevy, as if nothing more need be said. But the advantages of high status to an animal that does not compete for resources are by no means obvious. Many feral horse researchers do not see any possible advantage of high status within a band.

*Practices*

Horses have low aggression rates while grazing, so collecting enough data to construct a hierarchy can be a long and tedious process. To speed up the process by raising aggression, horses may be obliged to compete for food or water: Tyler, for instance, gave each group a little pile of hay; Stevens (1988) closed off all water sources on an island, leaving a hole from which only one horse at a time could drink. In the most extreme example, the bucket test, two hungry horses are given one bucket of food. Not surprisingly, the most aggressive wins.

That the bucket test should be thought to reveal natural social relations is astonishing, surreal, like studying family relationships by watching boxing matches. Nevertheless, what unleashed the obsessive search for equine dominance hierarchies and their significance was precisely a bucket test study.

In 1978 Houpt and others, given twenty thoroughbred yearlings, took two at a time, deprived them of food for eighteen hours and set them before one bucket of concentrates. Working through every possible pairing, they ranked winners and losers. A year later they repeated the process and found almost the same rank order. A characteristic of dominance hierarchies is that they are stable, to perform their function of reducing aggression. Therefore, the proposition was that this stable winner-loser order must be a dominance hierarchy. (The fact that the horses fought, in one-off contests, was overlooked.)

Hence 'horses have strict dominance hierarchies', and the hunt for their social relevance was on.

Craig, in 1961, had already criticized the idea that putting non-competitive animals in competitive situations reveals anything about their natural social relations, but few listened to him. The bucket test and its like were a fast track to results. Later, both Carranza (1995) and Coté (and teams) showed that in deer and feral goats, putting high-quality food in a pile disturbed their natural social relations entirely and changed their social organization radically. Grazing and browsing animals have not evolved social systems that curb aggression in competitive situations, because these situations do not arise in their natural lives. Their social relations go awry when faced with this unnatural, imposed challenge. Bucket tests do not 'reveal the hierarchy' as is claimed: they create one.

*Unacceptable parallels*

This means, of course, that there is no parallel between the social relations of feral horses and those of domestic horses, although there is assumed to be. In Table 2, I threw together results from feral horses, managed herds and domestic horses, because that is what is usually done. It is not justifiable. Feral horses live in bands of their own choosing, have no restriction on space (except on islands), and no competition for resources. Domestic horses live in a wide range of conditions. They do not choose their company; they are restricted for space; they do not breed naturally; and they usually have supplementary feed in piles or buckets. They are more like zoo animals than wild ones. We already know the hazards of drawing conclusions about social life from zoo animals. Mech and Boitani (2003), studying wild wolves, have shown that the conclusions drawn about wolves' and dogs' social behaviour from captive animals are a complete distortion of natural social relations.

## Other Issues

Before moving on to re-interpreting the results of equine dominance studies, I have a couple more reservations about the 'horses have strict dominance hierarchies' idea.

*'The' hierarchy*

Ellard and Crowell-Davis (1989), studying a group of domestic brood mares, measured dominance hierarchies in different situations, all normal in these horses' lives: grazing, eating at a hayrack, and eating from buckets, one per horse.

The hierarchies did not correspond.

There is no such thing as 'the' hierarchy. Hierarchies differ according to the situation. If you always watch the same group in the same situation – coming in to feed, for instance – you will see the same hierarchy, but if you watch them in other situations it will not be the same.

This calls into question whether what we are seeing is a dominance hierarchy for, according to Drews' definition, the relations are consistent. Ethologists get round this one by saying that hierarchies are context-dependent. Two factors are usually ignored. Firstly, not all aggression (etc.) has to do with conflict, although all enters into rank scores. Secondly, animals' individual motivation varies according to the situation. Some horses, especially ones who have known hunger, are more highly motivated by food than others; lactating mares are more highly motivated by water than others. Their insistence on reaching a resource before others varies according to the resource.

'The' hierarchy, like the $\alpha$ mare, is a myth, a shape-shifter.

*Dominance hierarchy or avoidance order?*

Dominance hierarchies constitute social orders that diminish aggression. Therefore, a group with a well-developed hierarchy should not show aggression during competition any more than at any other time. Subordinates should know their place and wait their turn.

Table 3 shows the results of studies that compared aggression rates in groups of horses while feeding in different situations. Since scoring methods vary, I have put each team's results in a different colour.

**Table 3   Aggression Rates/Horse/Hour in Different Feeding Situations**

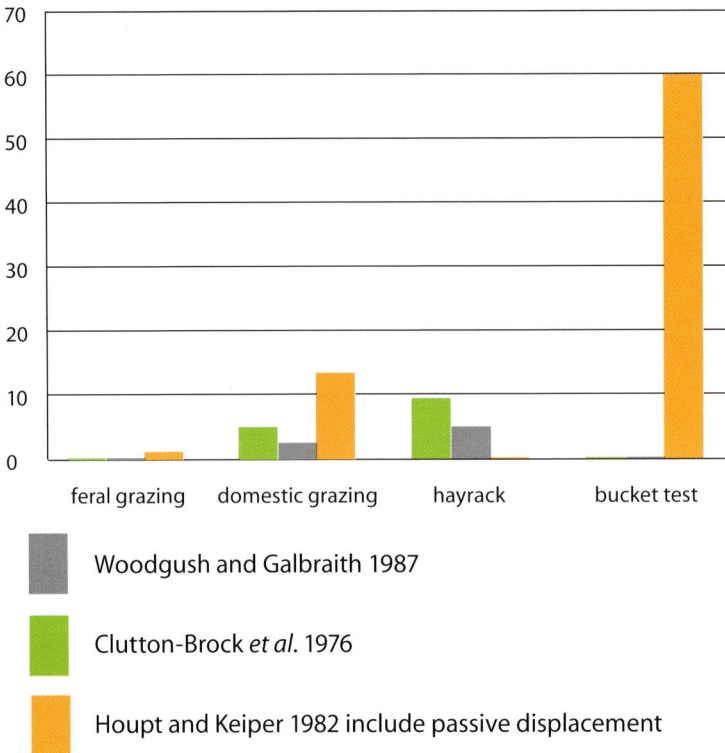

Woodgush and Galbraith 1987

Clutton-Brock *et al*. 1976

Houpt and Keiper 1982 include passive displacement

The 'feral grazing' counts of two teams are vanishingly small.

Clearly, the more competition there is, the more aggression there is, contrary to the expectations given by the characteristics of dominance hierarchies. Worse, in the bucket test, the researchers commented that the aggressions were far fiercer. While grazing, their group rarely did more than lay ears back or avoid another's approach. In the bucket test they flew at each other with savage bites and kicks. These horses had lived together for eight years, so each should have known their place in the hierarchy if such a thing existed. They didn't. Far from submissively knowing their place, the losers came back again and again, to be attacked ferociously each time.

This is not a dominance hierarchy. It is a bun-fight that the most aggressive wins.

For this reason Fraser (1992) proposes that what sometimes develops when grouped horses are routinely fed together is an avoidance order, in which horses who are aggressed (may) learn to leap aside before getting hurt. It is not a dominance hierarchy, because the aggressors do not reduce their aggression, though fast evasion leads to damage limitation. The order is maintained by avoidance, not by dominance. Jenson (1982) found the same in pigs.

Changing the name of what we see does not change what we see, but avoidance order does describe it more correctly than dominance hierarchy, as well as freeing it from the implications of authority, superiority and attractiveness that the word dominance carries. 'Dominant' horses are not attractive as dominant chimps are. They are avoided, even in the field, as Arnold and Grassia showed in an early study.

## RE-INTERPRETING DOMINANCE STUDIES

None of this exempts me from the task of explaining why some horse aggress and/or are avoided more than others.

I split studies into different categories: those on feral horses, on managed free-living herds and on domestic horses, for the social dynamics of each are different according to group composition and competition. Sometimes I cannot avoid using the terms dominant, subordinate and rank as researchers do, to avoid such clumsy circumlocutions as 'the horse who scores highest in a multiple scoring system involving aggression, threat, and being avoided', although the latter is what I mean.

## Feral Horses

In feral horse studies, dominance is used in descriptions of a variety of completely different social interactions.

1. Interactions between two bands, as in Miller's waterhole study (1979) where big bands, often multi-male, took precedence over small ones. Up to fourteen bands stand in line.
2. Interactions between stallions that affect the whole band, as in Rubenstein's study of band displacement from small patches of good grazing: the subordinate moves his band when he sees a dominant stallion's band coming.

These two show genuine dominance-submission relations, for after they have been established aggression is reduced and the dominant wins the resource.

3. The relationship between stallions in some multi-male natal bands, where one does not allow the other(s) to mate with mares. Subordinates, though, tend not to accept submissively; thus aggression rates may be high (Linklater) or not (Feh) depending on the population.

In conflictive interactions stallions do not use the same signals as those used in normal band interactions to signal social annoyance; instead of head-thrusts or rump presentation they are more likely to make displays of neck-arching, prancing (passage), foreleg strikes or stamping, squeals, and ritual dunging, as well as real fighting, with rears, neck-biting, leg-biting and so on. Apart from the dunging (which establishes identity for future reference), they use display moves in courtship as well, when mares also often stamp or give foreleg strikes.[36] In conflict, then, they display and/or fight, and these sequences can establish dominance-submission relations.

In contrast, when getting rid of annoying bachelors they chase or bite (unless the bachelor feels strong enough to try a real stallion fight), and are more likely to use the 'go away' signals of head-thrust, charge and bite to subordinate stallions when disputing access to mares. I feel that lumping display moves with 'go away' signals is not justified.[37]

4. Individual relationships within natal bands, my main concern here.

In natal bands aggression/threat rates are very low: between 0.1 and 0.25 aggressions/horse/ hour, depending on the scoring system (Berger, Houpt and Keiper). Most of these are ears-back, head-thrust, rear-end threat, threat to kick, and passive displacement, though mares sometimes get stuck rump to rump in mutual kicking bouts from which neither can disengage without receiving a full-strength kick.

Many feral horse researchers (including me) do not see dominance hierarchies within bands. None of the early studies mention dominance hierarchies; Feist and McCullough, Salter and Hudson, Rubenstein, Kimura and Berger say that dominance relations within bands are not noticeable. Many cannot see any possible function for them in a non-competitive society with low aggression and strong natural selection against it. Berger, who painstakingly collected the relevant figures over years, saw that the rank of any animal fluctuates: a mare will drive others away when she has a small foal, but when the foal grows she does not, so her rank apparently drops. A newcomer to a band gets aggressed by others, so her alleged rank is low; but when the band accepts her the aggression stops, so her rank apparently rises. When we consider the proximate causes of aggressions, the social annoyances that provoke them, instead of considering all aggression as related to dominance and winning conflicts, the reasons for apparent changes in rank become clearer. Many studies do not observe over a long period, so fluctuations may not show.

However, if data on threat and avoidance are collected and arranged in a hierarchy then what results is a hierarchy.

In all feral horse studies, rank in the hierarchy is closely correlated to age, as it is in other herd animals like bison and deer (Lott 1991).

The reason becomes clear if we look at proximate causes of aggression/threat mentioned in various studies.

**Table 4   Proximate Causes of Aggression in Feral Horse Bands while Grazing**

| Cause | Source | Age effect?[#] |
|---|---|---|
| Reject stallion (anoestrous mare) | Berger 1986 | no |
| Reject in-band colt (mare) | Kasewa and Nosawa 1996 | yes |
| Reject oestrous daughter (stallion) | Berger 1986 | yes |
| Reject in-band colt's attention to daughter (mare) | Monard *et al.* 1996a | yes |
| Proximity/ invasion of space* | Heitor *et al.* 2006 | yes |
| Reject new band member | Monard *et al.* 1996b | often |
| During mutual grooming** | Tyler 1972 | no |
| During play** | McDonnell and Haviland 1995 | no |
| During nursing** | Crowell-Davis 1985 | yes |
| Reject weaned foal (mare) | Berger 1986 | yes |
| Protect new foal (mare)*** | Keiper and Sambraus 1986 | yes |

**Key:**

#Age effect? Are aggressions in this group consistently given by older (i.e. mature) members to younger ones?

*Includes passive displacements

**Aggressor protests at being bitten

***Almost always driving away playful or inquisitive youngsters

On the whole, and for perfectly good reasons, mature horses threaten younger ones more than the other way round. Therefore, 'rank' will correlate to age.

Younger horses can and do threaten older ones too. If looked at in terms of hierarchy, these are called 'up-hierarchy' aggressions. Theoretically, these should not occur: subordinates should not threaten dominants, but "rank" is practically synonymous with age. If we think of the players as being younger or older rather than subordinate or dominant, the problem disappears.

Remembering the vital importance of collision avoidance gives a functional cause to irritation at invasion of individual space. Respect for individual space is a lesson driven home to youngsters, not as a demonstration of the power of the dominant to move the subordinate, but in the interests of survival during flight.

Correlations to high 'rank' seen in feral horses include success in breeding better foals, success in breeding future successful stallions (Feh 1990) and (sometimes) leadership. Again, when we substitute age for rank, the reasons become clear. Mature mares are better breeders than young ones; their sons grow better; and mature, lactating mares usually initiate water marches. When the hierarchy is split, as it is in some studies, into a top-half 'dominants' and a lower-half 'subordinates', the former will be mature mares and the latter younger. Rank then also correlates somewhat to size. Stevens' (1988) discovery that, at her one-horse water hole, dominants shoved subordinates aside (yes, they shoved) becomes self-explanatory if the 'dominants' were lactating and the 'subordinates' not, although she fails to mention these facts. So, too, the finding that stallions prefer dominant mares (in a free-living breeding herd) (Asa et al.1979). They are better breeders, being mature.

Many studies do not mention age, for the simple reason that the only quick way to determine the age of a feral horse over about three years is to anaesthetize the subject, not an easy procedure. Threats and displacements can be counted without interfering. Unless the population is well known, as the Assateague ponies are, or the study covers years, age is at best an informed guess. So correlations are often made to rank without attempts to make the same correlations to age. Berger did, and concluded that rank is, in the terms of Occam's razor, not a necessary entity. Rank explains nothing that age does not do better.

## Managed Free-Living Herds

These are characterized by colt-culling, reduced stallion/mare ratio, and winter feeding, although they are free-roaming and choose their own company. Many bands are small, a mare or two with foals and female offspring.

The effects of living without a stallion were shown in an Icelandic study that compared groups of brood mares with and without stallions. With a stallion, mares interacted little, aggressions were low, a dominance hierarchy could not be seen and mares did not mutually groom each other. Without a stallion, mares interacted more, aggressions rose, a dominance hierarchy could be seen (that is, some were consistently more aggressive/avoided than others) and mares mutually groomed (Granqvist *et al.* 2012). Our figures show that stallions are involved in two-thirds of a group's total interactions, including grooming mares and youngsters. Thus, mares without a stallion seem to be bothered by his absence and seek social interaction with each other more, but do not always find it satisfactory. Some ('dominants') were more irritated than others, who learned to leave them alone.

In managed herds where winter feeding is given, weight and size may correlate with rank more than in feral herds, an indication that food competition changes social relations as it does in deer, goats and cows. When Tyler was measuring dominance in her New Forest ponies, she gave them piles of hay to provoke aggression. These ponies also compete for visitors' handouts and goodies in the garbage, as do the Assateague ponies. In both these populations, dominance does not relate to age as clearly as it does in feral horses. It relates to size and weight too. In fights for food, the strongest and heaviest are likely to win; they learn that aggression pays, and become more aggressive in competition. The smallest and weakest lose, and learn to avoid the aggressors. This learning, called winner effect and loser effect (Dugatkin and Earley), is the basis of the development of an avoidance order.

Managed herds provided early studies on whether dominants initiate or end mutual grooming bouts, or whether subordinates do (a couple more studies give figures too). Nobody agrees on anything (Clutton-Brock *et al.* 1976; Tyler; Stebbins; Kimura 1998). The question reveals a peculiar interest in paralleling horses' social relations to those of chimps and other primates. But horses' mutual grooming is a symmetrical, synchronous dyadic activity, quite unlike that in primates, where one usually sits passively while the other grooms.

## Domestic Horses

Domestic horses live in a wide variety of situations and conditions, from extensive pasture to little, overcrowded patches; from isolation cells to family groups. One common factor is that aggression rates, though variable, are far higher than in feral or even free-living horses, even during grazing (*see* Table 2). The Highland ponies, a stable group grazing on the hill in relative freedom, had an aggression rate of 1.9/horse/hour compared to 0.1 with similar measures for feral horses. In competition for focal food – buckets, or piles of hay – aggression soars.

To investigators and horse-owners alike, aggressive competition for food focuses such a spotlight on win-lose relations that, like a torch beam on a dark night, it obliterates a wider-range vision of equine society. In this narrow beam the overriding factor in social relations becomes rank, although correlations to rank are notoriously inconsistent between studies.

In domestic horses, rank tends to correlate more to size and weight than to age, an indication that whatever sort of hierarchy we are calculating is not the same as that constructed from feral horse data. High-ranking horses win food competitions, which are often used to determine rank, a tautologous procedure. Some find they have bigger foals, who copy their mothers' models of social relations at least until weaning (Weeks *et al.* 2000). They are avoided; they are not leaders. Stallions, although the strongest, most agile and best fighters, do not rank high (Houpt and Keiper 1982). Rank does not, despite many investigations, correlate to learning ability in any form (Haag *et al.* 1980; Mader and Price 1980). High-ranking horses are not superior beings; they are simply more aggressive unless others learn to give them a wide berth. Some studies find that friends, or horses who mutually groom, are close in rank (which may be interpreted as meaning that they are the only pairs who have not learned to aggress or avoid each other).

Aggression in competition does not decrease, but increases in both frequency and ferocity. However, in some small, stable groups careful management can reduce aggression by teaching horses to file quietly to their own consistently placed buckets, giving the impression that they 'know their place in the hierarchy'. Move the buckets and the impression disappears.

In the usual feed-time fights the most aggressive do not control resources, since there is a bucket or pile of hay for each horse. So why do they persist in their aggression?

Switching off the dominance-focused spotlight allows two often-ignored factors determining the patterning of aggression to be seen: learning and stress.

*Learning*

Food is a potent reward. It is even more potent when horses have spent hours with empty bellies, a situation that does not occur in their natural lives. Concentrates, the reward value of which is often enhanced by appetizers, are super-potent rewards.

Focal food invites displacement, for two horses cannot feed together in one spot without invading each other's individual space, an equine transgression unless they be firm friends or used to huddling. Aggressive displacement is rewarded: the aggressor wins the food. The loser gets hurt, and is more liable to avoid conflict the next time. The relationship becomes ever more polarized as the situation is repeated. These winner effects and loser effects are seen throughout animal societies where repeated contests for resources occur.

Horses, even when fed by themselves, vary in their greediness for concentrates. For others, filling their bellies with hay is an overriding concern. Some are more particular about space invasion than others. So individual variation in motivation, apart from learning effects, gives reasons for horses to vary in aggressiveness from one situation to another – or, hierarchies are context-dependent.

Learning effects are also responsible for the non-linearity of equine hierarchies. In theory, hierarchies are linear if rank is, as treated, a measurable quality: each individual will be placed according to his measure. In practice they seldom are. Triangular relationships, as in D dominates E. E dominates F, but F dominates D, are common; so are much more convoluted circles and sub-circles. There is no puzzle to this if the relations are not about rank but the result of dyadic learning with potent rewards and punishments.

As any animal trainer knows, once an S→R connection has been established by strong rewards, it will strengthen with intermittent reward. When horses have learned to be aggressive to others in competition for food, they will continue to be so outside those situations – in the field, or in passing, for instance, one reason for high aggression rates during grazing. Learning is also responsible for that ultimately non-adaptive behaviour often seen in feed-time fights, when one horse, often a mare, suddenly leaves her food and flies to attack another. The S→R connection tells her that, at the sight of that horse feeding, attack will be rewarded. And she is right, again. The fact that she is wasting time and energy abandoning her own food does not occur to her.

Charlotte Hemelrijk is a computer animator interested in the spatial distribution of primates, whose food may be focal and so invite competition (this depends on the species). She gave her simulated 'animals' three calculations to guide their decisions, an algorithm, about whether to attack in competition: the gain in attacking, the risk involved in losing, and the inherent tendency to attack at a certain distance. When all three have high values, as in captive chimps, the 'animals' arrange themselves in concentric rings round a central dominant according to status, as they do in real life. By changing the values of the three components according to the species' natural lives – for instance, leaves have a lower gain value than rich fruit, some primates have bigger canines than others so the risk is greater – she successfully mimics the spatial distribution of real primate species. Adding learning effects stabilizes the situation.

When horses compete for focal food, their decisions as to whether or not to attack are guided by the same components of gain, risk, and attack tendency. A competitive algorithm is super-imposed upon Reynolds' flight algorithm, their natural guide. High gains increase aggressions: rates are higher in concentrate feeding than round hayracks. Risks are lower for the strong. Aggressiveness increases with motivation: when buckets appear, horses who have passed the night in a bare enclosure are more aggressive than those on good grazing. When grazing they are mainly guided by the flight algorithm, though habitual aggression learned in competition is also visible, depending on how much competition they experience in additional feeding. The exact conditions in which rank is calculated affect how much horses are guided by the imposed competitive algorithm and how much by the natural flight algorithm. The exact conditions in which they live and learn, and even their past experience in competition, will also be influential. Calculations made in different bands will not give consistent results.

*Behavioural stress*
Reward learning in food competition increases aggressiveness, but it is not the only reason for domestic horses' high aggression rates.

Domestic horses do not live in natural conditions. They do not choose their own company. Many lack the social education given by growing up in naturally composed groups. Groups change as horses are bought and sold. Mares rarely live with stallions. Space is restricted, sometimes drastically. Grouped horses may spend hours without food. Horses may be ridden in uncomfortable positions, bridles or saddles, and be in pain as a result. Their environments lack the stimulation of natural ones.

These factors provoke behavioural stress, the inability to adjust fully to abnormal environmental and social factors.

Stress affects different horses to different degrees, and with different effects: some get depressed, some get ulcers, some get allergies; some get over-attached to a friend. But a common effect is irritability. Stress makes horses aggressive, some more so than others.

Among its other pernicious effects, the dominance paradigm has detracted attention from an overall concept of social stress in domestic horses and its effect on their tempers. Aggression is seen as the strict enforcement of the 'dominance hierarchy', rather than the abnormal behaviour that it is. There is, however, a growing number of studies that link increased aggressiveness to living conditions, to stress and especially to social stress.[38] For instance:

1. Focal food competition increases aggression rates, as we have seen.
2. Fifty Arab mares turned out in a half-hectare bare paddock daily for six hours walked ceaselessly, did not roll or mutually groom, and only interacted aggressively. Given fifty haynets, they interacted, made friends, mutually groomed, rolled, and showed less aggression (Benhajali *et al.* 2009).
3. The smaller the enclosure, the higher are aggression rates in grouped horses (Jorgensen *et al.* 2009, Flauger and Kreuger 2013). In crowded conditions, avoiding invading others' space becomes difficult. Many studies on yarded cattle show the same.
4. Stebbins found more aggression in Appaloosas in paddocks than in pasture.[39]
5. How a youngster is brought up affects social skills. Adults teach youngsters social skills, punishing gaffs by driving offenders away. Bourjade and others (2008, 2009) showed that Przewalski youngsters brought up in a group without enough adults have higher aggression rates than those brought up in groups with natural adult-young ratios. The same has been shown in elephants (Bradshaw and Schore 2007). Unfortunately there is no similar research on domestic horses, who are often brought up in unnaturally composed groups in which aggression rates may be abnormally high.
6. Colts who had lived together and were then individually housed showed a sharp increase in aggression rates when released together again, an effect that gradually diminished (Christensen *et al.* 2002).
7. On Assateague, aggression rates are higher in bigger bands, where social interactions are more complex (Rutberg and Greenberg 1990).[40]

8. Group instability increases aggression, a common management problem. Feral horses aggress newcomers, too.
9. A dominance study on domestic mares and foals found that foal rank followed mare rank. When the foals were group weaned, aggression rates rose sharply and 'the hierarchy changed': that is, translated, there were individual differences in stress-related aggression in the foals (Weeks *et al.* 2000). Artificial weaning, even in groups, is never free of stress, which some foals feel more than others.
10. Foals intensively handled as neonates (so-called 'imprinting') were more aggressive to others as youngsters than foals whose first contacts with humans was voluntary (Henry *et al.* 2009). 'Imprinted' foals, whose handling has been imposed, are less sociable, less inquisitive, and more dependent on their mothers, an effect still noticeable in two-year-olds (and probably beyond that age).
11. Berger saw more aggression among mustangs living in the Grand Canyon of Colorado than among those in the Great Basin of Nevada. In the Grand Canyon, water is extremely scarce, and Berger concluded that the high aggression rate was a response to heat and thirst stress.
12. Mares in domestic situations usually live without stallions, which increases aggression between them (as mentioned above, Granqvist *et al.*).
13. Pain and discomfort increase irritability. A study of aggressive horses in riding schools found almost all suffering from back pain, some severely (Fureix *et al.* 2010). The degree of damage to the vertebrae correlated with aggression. These were stabled horses and the aggression was to humans.

Individual variation in responses to stress will reflect in rank measurements, just as individual learning effects do. With so many uncontrolled variables affecting outcomes, rank correlations will vary between groups. While it remains true that some horses are more aggressive, and others learn to avoid them, this has more to do with their individual histories, responses to stress and circumstances of measurement than to a conceptual quality of rank.

Rank is not an entity. It is a seductive mirage that vanishes the nearer we get to it, produced by the distortion of light and the shimmering haze of the heat of intense interest. Or, as that eminent primatologist Stuart Altmann had it, the Cheshire cat's grin.

## SOME CONCLUSIONS

*'Thinking within a fixed circle of ideas tends to restrict the questions to a limited field. And, if one's questions stay in a limited field, so do the answers.'* (David Bohm 1969)

From a standpoint outside that fixed circle, one sees a band of feral horses as a cohesive unit drifting from one activity to another in a synchronous flow that, at any moment, can be upgraded into a mass flight for survival. Until this happens, individuals are guided by the same factors that make flight possible: cohere, synchronize, respect others' space. These are modified by individual necessities as each animal completes its own role. There are no fixed leaders: any horse may suggest change, but band decisions to follow it are democratic, not despotic. There are occasional mild rebukes at errant youngsters, unwelcome courtiers and irritating neighbours, and male skirmishes over mares, but all differences disappear in the face of predators.

Feral horses have no dominance hierarchies within bands, nor any need for them.

Dominance-submission relations are sometimes seen between males, although they benefit the whole band rather than the individual. However, both these words have proved so peculiarly and powerfully attractive that they have been abused, for instance in describing one-off win/lose situations, courtship rejection, stallions' protective behaviour and reactions to discomfort.

Domestic horses experience stress, of different causes and degrees, that raises aggression rates. Competition for focal resources creates learning situations that also increase aggression and avoidance differentially until increasingly polarized relations are seen. Gain, risk and aggressiveness become influential in decisions about social reactions, overlying and masking the original flight algorithm to a greater or lesser extent, depending on the circumstances. The results do not conform to the theoretical properties of dominance hierarchies, but to learned avoidance orders. These vary within the same group in different situations.

As Drews said 'dominance is a concept, an intervening variable'. In the case of horses it has not proved a helpful one. It clarifies nothing about social relations, band structure or group behaviour in either feral or domestic horses, and has given rise to a great deal of muddled dogma. In the history of ethology, when certain words created similar confusion because of untenable claims and varied interpretations, they were dropped and replaced by clearer ones that did not carry the same resonances. 'Instinct' was one, 'drive' another. As far as equine ethology is concerned, dominance can go the same way.

## CHAPTER 8

# The Dominance Hierarchy Paradigm in the Horse World

Dominance has a particular fascination for the horse world, a hugely varied collection of sub-cultures that spans every social class in almost every country of the world. For the vast majority, horses are there to do what we want: pull water-carts, win competitions, herd cows, breed foals, attract admiration, perform circus tricks, be companions, slaves, therapists or personal challenges … the list is endless.

We use them. Whether we want to face it or not, the human-horse relation is one of power. The very act of keeping horses, even when we prefer to think of it as caring for them, means depriving them of liberty and choice. We subject them.

In some sub-cultures subjection is frank and brutal, and consciously so: since horses are stupid, being inferior to humans, only thwacks get through to them. Others realize that brutality terrifies horses, so favour the iron fist in the velvet glove approach. Constant control ensures they have little experience of acting under their own initiative, and resistance to our will meets pressure from the curb, the spur, the whip; depriving them of temptation and of learning opportunities when young helps render them submissive. A new approach is to use what are thought to be natural or 'ethological' parallels of equine social relations in training. According to ethologists, moving away from another horse signals submission. Therefore, if we chase them or prod them to move away they will naturally realize we are dominant over them and submit to our authority.

## MISINTERPRETING DOMINANCE

The ethological statement that horses have strict dominance hierarchies is most usually taken to mean that the imposition of authority from above is a social phenomenon shared by horses and us, one that they will naturally understand. 'Equine society and human society had enough in common to make domestication possible – a common "language" of dominance and submission that was intuitively and mutually intelligible … a common social fabric built upon both subordination to authority and trust.' (Budiansky 1997).

This statement, in an otherwise excellent book by a well-informed scientific writer (Budiansky was the American editor of *Nature* for years) shows the pitfalls of scientists' use of a common word according to their own specialized definition.[41] *The ethological concept of dominance is not what is generally understood by the word.* Correctly, most people understand the dictionary definition: supreme authority. The ethological definition is rarely given outside research papers, and even trained scientists sometimes have difficulty in restraining their interpretation of it to this narrow field.[42] Dominance is a word with powerful resonances. In the transcription of the concept first into textbooks, then into popular science-based books, into popular books and finally into that free-for-all of opinion, the Internet, a series of misunderstandings is created, as follows:

1. Any horse group has a strict hierarchy of authority.
2. Dominance is a character trait that leads to the dominant ruling the society.
3. Dominance, and therefore authority, is expressed and maintained by aggression.
4. Subordinates obey dominants.
5. When fighting, horses are working out the hierarchy or trying to rise in status. Similarly, when they resist us, they are trying to challenge our authority.
6. Therefore, in order to achieve submissive obedience from horses, exceeding firmness, to the point of hurting them, may be necessary to remind them of their position.

Unfortunately these fallacies are often perpetrated in books and by teachers who either do not know what ethological dominance is or are unable to dissociate it from authoritative dominance. This muddle results in sheer fantasy masquerading as scientific fact. We can look at these misunderstandings in more detail.

## 1. A Strict Authoritarian Hierarchy

Feral horse bands are widely believed to have an $\alpha$ dominant lead mare whom all who follow obey. Popularly the stallion is also dominant. 'Most horse families are composed of a single dominant stallion, the monarch, and a closely guarded harem of mares … (that) include a dominant female, the matriarch or lead mare.' (Jaime Jackson.) 'In equine society there is a leader, one horse which is the boss, and which the others respect and obey.' (Bayley and Maxwell). 'Horses are like humans, and many other creatures, in that they live by strictly-defined social rules and hierarchies, with a dominant herd individual.' (McBane).[43]

The parallels to human authoritarian hierarchies, seen also in the Budiansky quote, show the inevitable misunderstanding clearly. Note the enhanced, anthropomorphic language.

There is absolutely no evidence to suggest that horses have a concept of authority. It is an entirely human concept. If they did, we should not have so much trouble with them.

Nor, as we have seen, do they have leader dominant mares.

## 2. Dominance as a Character Trait

Popularly, dominance is not seen as describing a relation but as an inherent part of a horse's character, perhaps because highly self-assertive people are seen to have dominant personalities. For instance the Horse Personality Questionnaire, now used in research on human-horse relations, gives dominance as a major character trait (others are anxiousness, excitability, protection, sociability and inquisitiveness), adding that low dominance is selected in domestication (Lloyd *et al.* 2008). This implies that dominance has a genetic base.

Similarly the Parellis' guide to the 'innate personality' of the horse lists dominance as a characteristic of the 'left-brain horse'.

What the HPQ or the Parellis mean by dominance is impossible to understand, since they do not define it. Many people think that invasion of our personal space constitutes dominance rather than ignorance of social education; others think that poorly trained and badly ridden horses are dominant; others equate dominance with aggressiveness.

J.P. Scott, in early research on dominance, successfully taught 'dominant' mice to be submissive in encounters with other mice. Dominance is not a character trait, but expresses a learned relationship.

## 3. Dominance, Authority and Aggression

A dominant animal is not aggressive once relations have been established: that is precisely the difference between a dominant animal and one that wins fights. However a horse who is habitually aggressive to others is popularly called dominant. S/he is also seen as 'the boss'; s/he 'keeps the others in order'. That her only order is 'go away' escapes notice.

This identification of aggression with authority says more about the human mind than the horse's. A disturbing idea, it seems normal in many countries and cultures, though it is by no means universal.

Aggression is often confused with dominance: 'Aggression to people is seen most often in the stall …This is probably a form of dominance' (Houpt 1998). The author, recommends strapping the foreleg up to punish aggression and achieve dominance over the horse. In fact a horse's personal space occupies most of a stall, so that if the horse resents or fears aggressive intrusion into his space he must defend it since he cannot go away. Stallions, more sensitive to threat, are more prone to such defence and are often thought to be dominant, so that sometimes an escalating scenario of human threat and stallion defence ensues. In difficult cases, Houpt recommends shutting the horse in a stable without light, food or water, which are given only when the horse is visited. On the least sign of aggression, all are removed again. One can think of few ways to make a mad horse madder.

The confusion between dominance, aggression and authority has occasioned more illtreatment of horses, to the point of sending them to slaughter, and more injury to people, than any other single point in equestrianism.

## 4. Subordinates Obey Dominants

Submission, in its true sense, means ceding to another's will, not avoiding the other. Again, a semantic confusion originates in the ethological use of the word in a particular, incorrect sense in order to prop up the dominance-submission paradigm. The FEI (International Equestrian Federation), insisting that a ridden horse 'should show complete submission at all times', certainly does not mean that the horse should avoid his rider by throwing him off and escaping: that would be considered insubordination, not submission. There is no way to evaluate such behaviour using the dominance paradigm.

The FEI means the horse should accept his rider's body and be obedient to his aids. Obedience is a human concept. There is no indication that horses have such a concept, any more than they have a concept of authority.

What obedience means is that, at given signals, the horse invariably gives the responses regarded as desired. This is simple learning, as S-R theory shows. The obedient horse has been taught well. The 'disobedient' horse often has not, though his unwanted response may have other causes: physical inability, pain, fear, inappropriate or contradictory signalling being some.

Unlike dog trainers, horse trainers are largely unaware of learning theory. Horses usually learn by being pushed and pulled about until some of them guess what to do to avoid discomfort or pain – not a very scientific process. 'Natural' training has at least clarified the use of negative reinforcement (pressure-release), where in modern dressage, for example, constant inescapable pressure is the norm ('contact'). However 'natural' trainers, seizing on the ethological equivalence of avoidance to submission, often use repeated, forced avoidance to try to achieve the status that will apparently ensure the submissive obedience believed to exist in feral horses. The presumed hierarchical order seen on the march is paralleled by teaching the horse to follow the trainer. ('Horses obey the dominant leader.') As most horses have been carefully taught to walk beside the handler in the interests of safety, this often causes them some confusion, seen as their reluctance to accept their subordinate status.

## 5. Fighting is Working out the Hierarchy

This fallacy assumes that fighting is a normal part of social behaviour, not the result of poor welfare. 'In some situations, aggression is highly desirable, as when fighting takes place to establish a dominance hierarchy. The importance of such fighting is that once a hierarchy is formed, it provides … a means by which additional serious combat may be reduced.' (Houpt 1998). This is, of course, not true: combat is not necessarily reduced, as the author's own figures show (*see* Table 2) and horses get injured, sometimes fatally. The perception that fighting to establish 'the' hierarchy is normal, natural behaviour is precisely what keeps so many horses deprived of any social life at all, since owners fear injury. It has also deterred efforts to find reliable ways to minimize fighting.[44] In contrast, research on intensively housed farm animals has a vast, solid body of work free of such conjecture, to determine optimal trough space, group size and composition, forage provision and so on that minimize conflict and injury.

Introducing a new horse into an established group often provokes fighting. Feral horses reject newcomers too, but there are no fences trapping the newcomer. In domestic situations the newcomer is usually on unknown territory, insecure and defensive. Highly reactive horses provoke more fighting than calm ones. The measures found to reduce fighting – putting the newcomer and one of the group together in a new field, then introducing the group into it, for instance – do nothing to help the newcomer know his status: they merely reduce his defensiveness.

## 6. The Necessity of Keeping Them in their Place

Although hierarchies are said to be strict, horses are also said to struggle continually to improve their status (MacLean 2003). This contradiction is offered as an explanation for fighting. In our dominance-submission relations with them, then, we must expect from time to time that they 'try it on' and need reminding of their place, or status. A way of avoiding this is through constant control, never giving the animal any liberty of choice or movement. MacLean advocates careful teaching to bring responses under stimulus control, but in less enlightened circles this apparent resistance to authority may be broken down by painful devices and downright refusal met with punishment. Perhaps as part of our evolutionary legacy as predators, our natural reaction when trying to control a struggling animal seems to be to increase pressure on it.

## WHY THE MISINTERPRETATIONS?

This set of misunderstandings and fallacies causes a great deal of muddle that extends far beyond even what I have pointed out; suffering and bad practice result. The dogma that horses have strict dominance hierarchies appears to give scientific support to it. All the references given above appear in modern books in a University library section on equine science; some are textbooks written by ethologists.

Against this flood of misinformation some have made a stand: Fraser (1992), with his avoidance order, Marthe Kiley-Worthington (1987), who insists that dominance is only seen in unnatural conditions, and others. Recently there are signs that the flood is ebbing, that ethologists are tiring of trying to make head or tail of the monster they have created and are finally paying more attention to affiliative behaviour instead of conflict, to aggression as a management problem instead of a natural one. But the monster is out on the streets. The general public, haunted by it, lags far behind research swings unless and until they are put firmly into the public eye. The monster needs an official, public execution.

To be fair, not all the misapprehensions derive from scientific research that has tried to cram equine social behaviour into a pre-imagined form, presenting it in a manner open to misinterpretation. The picture itself seems to have a curious attraction, a fascination that blinds people to the evidence of their own experience. Thoughtful people since Xenophon have known that aggressive dominance produces no desirable results, yet aggression is widely identified with being 'the boss,' whose orders are obeyed. When Monty Roberts proposed that head-lowering signifies submission, many people believed him, although they saw daily that a timid horse cornered by an aggressive one does not lower his head: he gets out, or gets hurt. People want the dominance-submission picture to be the right one, and are prepared to pay for it by distorting their vision.

This invites the question 'why?'

## Bacon's Idols

In trying to sort out the numerous reasons why the dominance hierarchy paradigm should win such general acceptance despite its obvious contradictions and shortcomings, I found a scheme of the Elizabethan philosopher and scientist Francis Bacon helpful. Before setting out what he thought was the best approach to discovering the truth underlying any phenomenon, he first classified the reasons why this should be so difficult as to need careful explanation and method. He called these reasons idols, false gods that blind us and lead us astray, and listed four:

- *Idols of the tribe.* These are delusions common to all men, like accepting evidence that backs up our theory but ignoring that which does not; drawing universal conclusions from few examples; reifying abstractions; and what we might call anthropomorphism, the belief that our way of thinking about and classifying nature is the only right one.
- *Idols of the theatre.* These are learned delusions resulting from accepting received ideas and false demonstrations; accepting what we are taught without challenging it; cultural influences.
- *Idols of the marketplace.* These are fallacies arising from our use of particular words, like names of non-existent things that are supposed to exist merely because they have names,

and names of things recklessly applied to quite different things that superficially seem the same.

- *Idols of the cave*. These are personal prejudices arising from our particular point of view, a reference to Plato's metaphor of the cave.

Bacon's idols have proved to have permanent analytic value, unlike his scientific system (Descartes' was easier to follow and gave better results). I have given his points more or less as he put them and, even without sculpting them to my theme, they echo with chilling exactitude the criticisms I have levelled at the dominance hierarchy paradigm and the fallacious muddle it engenders. They also provoke the following thoughts.

### Idols of the tribe

Do we want to see social dominance hierarchies in horses because they are innate in humans? We are, after all, primates and, although the importance given to social dominance in primate societies has greatly diminished, they do seem to be the only animals in which the phenomenon exists at all. In other animals, dominance-submission relations are ritualized win-lose relations in defined circumstances, as in Rubenstein's Assateague stallions' ability to displace others from good grazing patches; in primates they have more pervasive social effects, for instance in the social spacing that Charlotte Hemelrijk's simulations investigated. Do we try to link 'rank' to other social behaviour just because our minds are constructed to do so?

Cummins, a developmental psychologist, has investigated deontic thinking in infants across an enormous range of nations and cultures. Deontic thinking is 'should/shouldn't' in social settings: for example, how to modify behaviour in the presence of a social superior. Jerry Fodor, in a brilliant little book *The Modularity of Mind*, has shown that we have quite different and separable ways of thinking, almost like computer programmes that process different types of information. Deontic thinking, like cause/effect thinking or theory of mind (knowing that what another person knows is not what you know), is a module. Cummins (1996) has shown that it develops in the human infant earlier than the other two mentioned, and is universal.

Deontic thinking is the basis of social dominance relations, the idea that what is appropriate behaviour depends on the importance of the person present. Whether or not deontic thinking develops into social hierarchy is a matter of culture: some cultures, like our present Western one or the Hindu caste system, accentuate and value social status; others, like the Navajo, eschew the very idea. But the basis for it seems there in our minds: they are pre-moulded to the idea of social hierarchy.

I find this idea just as disturbing as the popular equivalence of aggression to authority, or the prevalence of power relations, especially in horsemanship. These linked themes, which recur in the fields of psychology, anthropology, sociology and history, are of the type about which most of us theorize freely without sufficient background knowledge or training (as indeed is ethology), and some expert knowledge would greatly enlighten the path towards a truly informed horsemanship. Concentration on techniques of manipulation has led us to ignore the bases not only of horses' attitudes but of our own as well.

We have, in analytical thinking, a great tendency to dichotomize, to classify and to create hierarchies in our classification schemes, and to attach value judgements to those we classify as higher or lower. For many years the study of evolution was dogged by the idea of its being a ladder leading to the apical Us, with animals occupying higher or lower rungs. The tendency to rank winners and losers gives us an exaggerated interest in conflict. We and dogs rush to watch conflicts, but horses go away to more peaceful places. When stallions have conflictive encounters, mares are singularly uninterested, human observers enthralled. Television documentaries invariably exaggerate conflict behaviour: watching horses eat, sleep and walk about is 'boring'.

*Idols of the theatre*
The stage of the dominance drama is the domestic setting, not the feral one.

Equestrian teaching has two main roots: the military and the working traditions. In both, people interact on hierarchical authoritarian principles, which they tend to apply to horses. 'Teach the horse who's master' has been a guiding principle in both.

Classical dressage claims different aims, the creation of art. Its real flowering came in the eighteenth century, when the nobility left their country estates and hunting and moved to court. As swiping each other with swords developed into delicate fencing, so too riding lost its functionality and became refined into a gentleman's leisure pursuit. Foucault (1980) has shown that this period saw the foundation of institutions organized on authoritarian lines – schools, hospitals, prisons, orphanages, workhouses, factories, the military – all sharing the same characteristics: separating people so they could not interact; mindless drilling; punishment for laziness, errors or independent thought; an improvement of status as people moved up the ladder of systematic training; and a central, public exercise ground where supervision could be maintained. The aim of all these institutions was to produce 'docile bodies', productive, manageable units devoid of autonomous will. Classical dressage shows curious parallels, down to 'complete submission at all times'. Nowadays competition has corrupted even the lofty ideal of perfecting nature by art, de la Guérinière's aim, but retained much of the system and concepts that produced it.

Despite their great technical ability, the great classical masters lived before the solid body of experimentation that gave rise to learning theory, from which we derive our knowledge of how reinforcement and punishment work. To them, punishment, (or 'correction' as it is often euphemistically termed) teaches an animal to obey, and is thus a necessity, though one to be used sparingly, in the forging of the just master-willing servant relationship they envisaged creating. B. F. Skinner, learning theory's great master, genuinely believed that his results would eliminate the use of punishment in education and training, for he showed that punishment cannot teach an animal what to do. When we read the timeless advice of the old equestrian masters, we should remember that their values and understanding reflect those of past societies.

*Idols of the marketplace*
In equine ethology, misrepresentation of behaviour owing to the inaccurate, over-extended use of words is not confined to dominance, submission and rank but also to conflict, or agonistic, behaviour. When moves can be used in conflict, their use is presumed always to signify conflict. Thus stallion display behaviour and protests at being bitten are classified as conflict behaviour. Protective herding is also often seen as dominance, for the stallion moves others away. The first attempt at a partial equine ethogram, 'Agonistic ethogram of the equid bachelor band', described play between colts (McDonnell and Haviland).[45] Many of the moves described can be and are used in real fights, but in play the sequences are not carried to the point of injuring the other. To call them agonistic is to misrepresent their style and finality, thus encouraging inaccurate observation; their social significance is misinterpreted as a result.

Bacon criticized the reification of abstractions. Status or rank is presumed to exist because it has a name. Stuart Altmann, a primatologist, wrote: 'Dominance is an invention, not a discovery. Do dominance relations exist? Yes, in the mind and notebook of the human observer. Like the Cheshire Cat's grin, they are an abstraction, a discerned pattern …. Are dominance relations important? They surely are, but to the investigators, not to their subjects.'

In popular parlance, concepts of laziness, rebelliousness, resistance, cheekiness, self-will, naughtiness, goodness, obedience and so on permeate analyses of horse behaviour in our hands and influence the thoughts of hearers.

*Idols of the cave*
Although it may not appear so from the outside, the scientific community is a highly competitive one, status-ridden and insecure. Research grants are short-term, won by the merit of a scientist's work as measured by the number of publications and the number of times they are cited in other publications; its importance to mankind counts too. Scientists have critical, public conflicts with remarkably little personal acrimony compared to other societies, though they prefer the bloodless triumph of the self-evidently dominant.

From the popular point of view of the human-horse relationship, many are, whether they admit so or not, daunted by the sheer size and power of horses. The fear of loss of control (sometimes not just of horses) is a preoccupation for many. Others fear being made to look foolish when their animals or children misbehave in public. Horses have a way of exposing these fears.

Fear and frustration both provoke aggression. To be taught that aggression to horses is justified and necessary to maintain the required dominance over them is, then, highly satisfactory. Milgram's sobering experiments in the 1950s showed that the majority of people knowingly inflicted what appeared to be extremely painful punishment on others simply because they were told to do so during an experiment for which they had volunteered.[46] Later, he showed that those with a rigid, authoritarian personality structure did so with fewer qualms than others. To this type of person, the equine dominance paradigm has intuitive appeal, and it is what such people will teach.

There are many reasons why the dominance paradigm is easily accepted. None of them mean it is true.

## CHAPTER 9

# Changing the Paradigm

The proposition that social systems evolve as adaptations to natural selection pressures is not a new or revolutionary one: sociobiology is the study of such adaptations. Nor is the perception that horses are gregarious prey animals without competition for maintenance resources. What I am proposing is that we draw logical conclusions from these two statements: that during the evolution of horse social organization, predation pressure was a major influence, while the need to control aggression in focal resource competition was irrelevant. Testing and applying these conclusions involves a change in the present way of analysing what we see, both in research and in our daily treatment of horses: a paradigm shift.

## EQUINE ETHOLOGY

Ethologists are at last tiring of ranking horses into hierarchies and wondering what that means, and are turning to examining how we can keep them better. But the dogma of the dominance hierarchy remains despite its defects. Both in textbooks and in teaching, the flaws in methodology and evidence are passed over. Students should be taught to evaluate evidence critically, not to accept dogma. I have pointed out these defects at some length because I move and work in the horse world and am conscious of the ever-increasing hold that the dominance hierarchy paradigm has on the interpretation and treatment of horses. As people become less and less connected to the natural world, they are increasingly guided by popular science. Let this be clear, not open to misinterpretation, based on sound scientific principles and solid evidence.

In the light of new research on wild wolves by David Mech, canine ethologists have stated publicly, through statements on the Internet (AVSAB 2008) and revised teaching of applied ethologists and dog trainers, that their previous standpoint on dominance and submission in dogs was based on misinterpretation of certain gestures and signals. They have done so not simply because the new research promoted a different view – that happens all the time in science and goes without comment – but because they realized that dog welfare was compromised by punitive training schemes and treatment based on anthropomorphic interpretation of the dominance paradigm. Changes in attitude and interpretation take time to filter through to the general public, and canine ethologists have, in this way, accelerated the flow of better information, to the benefit of dogs and their owners.

The same kind of well-publicized revisionary statement from equine ethologists is necessary and indeed overdue, for the same reasons. Ethological statements about dominance are wholly misunderstood by the general public, to the detriment of horse welfare.

On a more positive and exciting note, the new paradigm opens many avenues of research, the first being in-depth analysis of band synchrony beyond my mainly qualitative observations. Quantitative analytical techniques have been developed in the investigation of synchrony, emergent or self-organizing movement and cohesion in other herd animals (for instance Engel and Lamprecht 1997), and the field is open to constant advances and developments. They have not been applied to horses except in Kreuger's study on leadership - in which, notably, the results support the self-organizing paradigm, not that of a dominance hierarchy headed by an α mare.

The self-organizing paradigm highlights the lack of investigation into why aggression rates in domestic groups are much higher than in feral bands. Since aggression has been primarily related to status, there is no body of work that evaluates it in terms of stress-related factors like living conditions, group size, group composition, group changes, exercise regimes, hunger, thirst, handling, use of reward and punishment, weaning, fear, pain, feeding regimes, or space when feeding, to mention but a few. There are, as previously cited, studies that show some of these links but in general research is scant, especially when compared for instance with the solid body of work that links stereotypes to behavioural stress. There is no overall concept of stress-related aggression, nor analysis of the relative importance and interaction of its contributory factors. Domestic horses are so variable in their responses and conditions of living (partly as a consequence of the complicating effects of varied social upbringing and history), that research must be repeated on many different groups before universal conclusions can be reached. Investigation into the role of reward learning in raising aggression rates will be fraught with the same difficulties.

Socially deprived domestic stallions often become over-anxious to reach others, for which they are severely punished, either deliberately or through the use of painful restraints like the Chifney. The anticipation of pain (ears-back, tail lashing) increases the popular impression that stallions are inherently aggressively dominant and are constantly trying to attack others. Further ill-treatment and isolation are likely to follow (Goodwin). There are no clear research-based guidelines for avoiding either aggressiveness or stress-related low fertility. In practice both improve greatly by making concessions to the stallion's natural role as protector, in which his overview and contact with others, especially sons, other entires or permanent mates, are important; but there is little research on the subject.[47]

Equally there is no research-based advice for architects designing new installations: their criteria are human-based, not equine.

## THE PRACTICAL HORSE WORLD: INTERACTING WITH HORSES

Our interactions with horses are a constant interchange of signals in which each acts according to his or her interpretation of the other. Horses perceive our signals with superhuman sensitivity and accuracy; we tend to be less observant and base our interpretations more on concepts like character, intention and what we imagine to be the horse's hidden agenda. Changing the paradigm means changing the interpretations that inform our actions.

The defence algorithm provides a basis to re-examine how we and horses move together. This is not to say that horses relate to people in the same way as they relate to other horses or other animals, but they do react to our movement in the same way. Brusque, aggressive movements startle horses, creepy predatory movements make them nervous, and calm, confident movements inspire their cooperation. We do already know this, but training ourselves into letting their algorithm be our guiding principle is another matter. Its components reveal how the concepts that underlie our management style can facilitate or complicate all our dealings with horses.

## Cohesion

Firstly, cohesion. Horses live in groups for their own safety. They live and move together, following each other's leads without resistance or resentment, because that way leads to survival. In the more or less unnatural world we surround them with, their safety in our hands forms the basis of a naturally attractive relationship for them, one that invites voluntary cooperation.

They are, of course, prey animals. We constantly underestimate the delicacy of their perceptions and feelings on this matter. They do not feel safe when we trap them and impose control on them, especially when that control involves discomfort to the point of pain. They do learn to avoid discomfort, but their natural basis for moving together voluntarily is the safety that others' company represents, not the avoidance of discomfort or aggression.

From the horse's point of view, the safety of a band lies not only its physical shielding but also the communication network it represents. Horses perceive and react to each other's signals. We tend to ignore or override their attempts to communicate with us. We may not agree that such and such an object is dangerous or that it would be more agreeable to eat grass right now, but to have one's communications constantly ignored or met with disagreeable treatment does not engender willingness and cooperation in them any more than it does in us. As Xenophon knew, when a horse is afraid, he loses his fear when we show him we have seen the problem but are not afraid: punishing fear with discomfort and pain increases fear. As de Pluvinel knew, a young horse's sweet interest is like the scent of a flower: once lost, it does not return. When we banish them to the realms of non-communication we isolate them.

Horses' natural channels of communication are visual signals like social gestures, body attitudes, movement and position relative to each other;

Fig. 9.1  *When we understand the principal of herd movement, we have the confidence to allow the horse to make his own decisions and learn for himself.*

auditory ones like calls, stamps and hoofbeats; smells and pheromones; taste, when they use their lips, and touch in soft attention-seeking nudges and affiliative social interactions. They do not use physical pressure and release in prods and pulls, although this is often taught as the major or sole method for us to communicate with them. Within a band, horses are continually aware of others' body attitudes and position. Being more verbal and goal-oriented, people are often unaware of their position, movements and gestures: we can and do confuse horses by giving contradictory signals without realizing what we are doing. Confusion is incoherent, the antithesis of coherence.

For a horse, coherence and synchrony are interdependent: without coherence there is no synchrony. Before we can move on to inviting synchrony, then, our first consideration must be whether the horse wants to be with us. The best test is to give him the option in a space big enough for him to get away from us, without any bribes or pressure tactics but only our determination to learn what constitutes good and interesting company for a horse. A surprising number of experienced horsemen find that they do not even know how to touch a horse in a way that invites cohesion, though the hand is one of our greatest aids to seduction.

## Synchrony

What induces horses to follow and synchronize with others is confident, purposeful leadership. Though fixed leaders do not exist, temporary leadership does: that is, it is a quality that both we and horses can show at one moment and lack at another. A mare who wants others to accompany her marches off in a determined way, checking to see if others are following. If they are not, she comes back and invites them again. She has no way of obliging them to follow her. Horses readily learn to transfer this following reaction to us without being pressurized into doing so. Since we are not horses, we may have to repeat our invitation several times at first until the horse realizes that the same synchronizing response is as appropriate

Fig. 9.2 In natural, synchronous play, no pressure is necessary. These games in early training (the horse is a three-year-old stallion destined for classical dressage) engage the horse's voluntary cooperation.

and satisfactory with us as it is with other horses: that is, there is certain amount of learning in the situation, as Kreuger (2007) found. Nevertheless, learning to synchronize with us as they do with other horses comes far more naturally to them than learning how to react to pressure on a rope. The exercise also teaches us to move appropriately. If we want a horse to move, we must move; if we want a stop, we must stop. Once we know how to invite cohesion and synchrony, ropes become largely irrelevant.

Synchrony, moving as one, flowing together without coercion, is the highest aim of any kind of horsemanship, and its greatest pleasure. Horses are natural synchronizers, to the point that once they want to be with us they copy our steps on the ground and respond to the signals of intent in our bodies when we ride them. The concepts of synchrony and harmony in riding are increasingly being used by modern teachers who have found them central to a horse's voluntary cooperation, possibly without having realized their survival value.

We tend to underestimate the horse's sensitivity to the body's movements of intention and his willingness to synchronize with them: dressage riders sometimes become frustrated by a horse's 'anticipating' a movement before they have consciously asked for it, for merely thinking about it produces tiny body changes that can give the horse enough information to act on. The horse responds to our body changes by making the same changes himself. At its simplest this involves turning the head or shoulders so that the horse turns, or stopping the flow of our body with his movement so he stops, the way any stockman does. A thoughtful stockman discovers how to use his body so effectively that his movements are barely perceptible and reins are unnecessary. This is not a matter of sophisticated riding instruction but of self-correcting experimentation: to the horse, every body is a different combination of weights and balances with which he naturally synchronizes if they are coherent. He is such an adroit synchronizer that he changes the fine details of each part of his body according to what we are doing with the corresponding part of ours, the basis of the aids.

In using the aids we invite the horse to change what he is doing with a certain part of his body by making that change with the corresponding part of our body. To ask him to move his legs we move ours. To ask him to step outwards with a forefoot we move our hand outward. To invite a shoulder-in we turn our shoulders as we wish him to do, keeping the pelvis straight. When he canters on the left lead we both have the left hip slightly in front of the right; to invite a flying change we switch the inclination of our pelvis while he is in mid-air so he does the same, landing with his pelvis correctly aligned to strike off on the other lead. Aids are invitations to synchronize. Like the horse who wants others to follow, we may have to repeat our invitations with vibrating aids. If we apply them with increasing, rigid pressures the horse responds by becoming rigid too.

The greatest impediment to this harmonious, united flow is tension, either in ourselves or in the horse. Blocking any part of our body makes the horse do the same. The rider's first challenge is to find tension-free synchrony with the horse's movements, to become a part of the flow without trying to influence it. Only then, when the horse's fluid movement is not impeded, can he synchronize with the small changes that the rider makes. A moment's thought shows that if we are trying to influence where a horse will step next – say, we would like his right hind foot to step to the left instead of straight ahead – we must time our suggestion to coincide with his ability to follow it. In this case we must move our right foot to the left while his right foot is in the air, for if he is standing on it he must simply ignore our ignorant demand. Being able to feel the horse's body as if it were our own, and move our own as if it were his, requires a complete lack of tension, for tension blocks sensitivity. Constant pressure is tension: against the rein pressure that many riders think is 'contact' the horse must push rigidly in order to advance, and this rigidity makes him inflexible.

*Fig. 9.3 The aids are also invitations to synchrony: the more lightly we apply them, the lighter the response.*

Changing the paradigm means changing the way that riding is taught. Riding is not a contest for control but a search for synchrony.

Analysis of synchronous activity in animals showed motivation to be an important factor. Although synchrony with others is his default setting, a horse who has reasons not to do what they are doing does not synchronize with them. We must expect, then, that leading or riding through synchrony alone will work most of the time but not always. Two questions arise: how can we increase the motivation to cooperate, and how do we react in the heat of the moment?

## Motivation

*Positive motivation*

'Flexibility and lack of obligation are pre-conditions for any voluntarily-offered obedience that is neither martyrdom nor slavery for the horse.' De la Guérinière.

'Training a horse does not mean achieving his submission, as is so often said: it also means making sure that the horse enjoys doing what is asked.' Nuno Oliveira.

Motivation preoccupied the great masters, none of whom used pressure and force, advocating delicacy, kindness and empathy. These principles apply even at the most basic levels. We cannot annihilate the horse's will in uncomfortable basic exercises and expect him to perform willingly at higher technical levels.

Motivation can be innate, learned through reward training, or a mixture of the two. If we put a horse in a situation where he wants to do something and ask him to do it, he will. We are then in the happy position of being able to reward his response to our signals: that is, we use innate motivation to facilitate the willing response, and learned reward motivation to create a firm, habitual S→R link.

For instance, when I first ride a young horse, I have a helper who walks ahead. Uncertain what to do in this novel situation, the horse naturally follows the helper, his security. I ask for turns, stops and starts a split second before my helper makes them, so the horse responds correctly. I say 'good' and caress his withers briefly. Within minutes he has learned the favourable response to my indications (mostly body) and no longer needs the helper. Gradually the learned motivation replaces the innate.

This idea can be applied at all levels of training. In classical, Pavlovian conditioning, where a new stimulus elicits a response, the trainer begins by ensuring there is a natural way of eliciting the response (in Pavlov's dogs, showing them a piece of meat to elicit salivation) before coupling the new stimulus (the bell) with the response. We do the same: we put the horse in a situation where he responds naturally before asking him to do so on application of our stimulus.

A frequent problem is lack of impulsion, the will to go forward. A young horse is unlikely to develop true impulsion going round in circles in a featureless enclosed patch of desert, and even more unlikely to do so with constant pressure on the reins, a drop noseband clamping his mouth shut and the rider's legs nagging his sides. Where he is lively and forward-going is out exploring the countryside, for which he needs supporting company like an understanding, fluid rider confident enough to leave his mouth alone. He takes months to re-balance himself and find, on uneven ground, that he can be as agile ridden as unridden; he strengthens himself willingly climbing hills and banks; becomes supple weaving in and out of trees; discovers on downhill slopes how to take his weight on to his hind feet, naturally collecting

*Fig. 9.4 When a horse is physically well prepared, the knowledgeable use of slopes helps him master difficult movements like piaffe more spontaneously than does flat ground.*

himself. In time impulsion becomes habitual to the extent that when we put him in the school he does not lose it, and recognizes what we are asking for when we ask it. All this time he has enjoyed himself and been rewarded for his efforts.

Without the possibility of country rides we have to use more imagination to create interesting situations that spark the horse's curiosity, making the back yard into a series of agility problems and using obstacles, labyrinths and cones to create motivation.

At the highest level, my friend Delia Daniels, an artist at traditional Spanish high school, uses banks and slopes so imaginatively and skilfully that when a horse is strong and well-balanced enough he naturally offers her piaffe and passage – spectacularly, since he is doing it for the best of reasons, to display his strength and agility.

When he is made uncomfortable, hurt, afraid, blocked by the rider's tension or subjected to constant pressure, a horse lacks any motivation except to escape the situation. He switches off his attention when our attempts to communicate are ill-timed, contradictory or inconsequential, just as he ignores rabbits. He cannot be motivated by the exclusive use of negative reinforcement, that is, making him uncomfortable until he moves to liberate himself from pressure. He learns, but does not enjoy the process of learning. Positive reward, that word of praise and small caress, does motivate, so that when teaching a new response through the use of negative reinforcement we use rewards to reinforce the response and motivate the horse to enjoy trying again.

*Conflicting motivation*

When I ride my stallion past fields of mares his interest in synchrony disappears, replaced by strong motivation to leap the wall and frolic with the fillies. In such situations we must use well-established, learned S-R signals. Pulling at the reins produces synchrony in that he pulls back. The effective use of the reins is blocking.

When a small foal wants to suckle and his mother is walking ahead, he gallops ahead and blocks her, swinging his body across her chest. When she stops, he dives for the udder. Horses understand blocks. Blocking with the reins means keeping the hands still and firm as stone. If the horse wants to pull against us, that is his problem: we do not apply the pressure, he does. When he realizes he cannot go forward and cedes, that is the moment to ask for synchrony or responses to aids. In this situation I often ask the stallion for passage, since he will do it willingly to impress the mares. Thus we are united again.

Changing the paradigm means changing the way we analyse situations in which the horse does not cooperate with what we think we are asking. Why would he prefer to do something else? Knowledgeable riding school horses are accused of 'trying it on' with inept riders, on the assumption that they recognize that the rider lacks authority. This is a complicated, dominance-based interpretation. The reality is simpler. When being ridden is a torture of tension, incoherence, prods and jabs the horse would prefer to stand by the door. Any animal would.

## Collision Avoidance

We do not want horses who barge into and over us.

Feral horses are taught collision avoidance by being shooed away angrily if they invade another's space or behave anti-socially within it. Domestic horses without herd upbringing are socially ignorant, and 'imprinting' teaches foals not to respect our space. Over-petting and feeding titbits diminish respect for space. However, a horse learns readily if we use the same technique as the mares. Leaving the horse loose in a space big enough to get away, we stop him a couple of paces away with a plastic bag on a stick. Only when we give a clear signal of relaxation may he enter our space and if he bites us playfully, as isolated colts do, out he goes again.

I hate this work, for although no physical punishment is inflicted, no horse should need to be corrected for the errors of foolish humans.

Respect for space works both ways. We should not invade the space of a horse in a stable until he gives us the signal that we may enter. Most particularly, we should not aggressively invade the space of a horse with a tendency to defend it.

We note that horses do not use punishment on each other except for hurting them or when 'go away' signals are not heeded. A mare does not punish her foal when he does not come to her call. Nobody is punished for not synchronizing, except by pumas. When we change the paradigm we punish less often and invite more frequently.

## Learning

Horses never stop learning from their experiences, even when we are unaware of it. Whether they learn what we want them to is a different matter.

Teaching involves knowing how to teach: studying learning theory, as other animal trainers do. Knowing how and when to reward; how to set up situations in which the horse will learn easily; how to use signals in a clear, consistent way; how to make learning interesting; how many repetitions are necessary to cement learning; when to stop; why horses learn something other than what is hoped for, and what to do about it – these factors mark the difference between good and bad teachers. Horses are often treated as if they really know the answer to what is asked, and have to be taught the obligation of doing it by being made increasingly uncomfortable, or punished, until they do. As is so often the case, the reality is far simpler.

*Fig. 9.5   Natural motivation enhanced by training engenders cognitive learning. This young mare has been introduced to cutting and now enjoys her expertise.*

They are animals, lost in our world, seeking to repeat pleasant experiences and avoid situations in which unpleasant ones occur.

## Maintenance

Horses cannot be expected to live in wholly unnatural conditions without suffering. Their extraordinary gifts, from which we can learn and benefit so much, do not flourish in conditions of deprivation. Many become depressed (which suits people who want to operate them like will-less automata), some become hysterical, others bad-tempered and yet others drug themselves through stereotypy. Unfortunately, many people have only seen them in these conditions and think that horses are by nature like that. Studying horses in natural conditions makes clearer what their fundamental necessities are: contact with others, communication, physical comfort maintained by free movement, rolling and stretching, and always something to nibble at, preferably green.

*     *     *     *

This exposition of what changing the paradigm means in practical terms is of necessity brief, for this is not a training manual. For some, the revelations given by the study of feral horses and their survival tactics will provide a wider, firm theoretical basis to what they have already partially discovered through their own sensitivity and experimentation; for others, taught that horses understand punitive, authoritative dominance, these ideas will be so wholly revolutionary as to be bewildering. Revolutions do not happen overnight, nor of their own accord, even when they are long overdue.

As society changes, so do its needs and interests. In the parts of the world most likely to read this book the horse now has little practical function except in police work and therapy, though many make their living from horses. Their main function is our amusement: for betting, competition, pleasure riding, companionship, or the fascination of interacting with an alien form of being. These would seem the best reasons to try to understand and treat them without damaging them.

In the field of therapy, horses are often said to act as mirrors to people. The vision of their society as competitive, hierarchical and aggressively status-seeking reflects the worst qualities of our society, but is a distorted one. A truer vision reflects our better qualities: immense sociability, the ability to respect each other's living space and style, delight in harmless playfulness, the capacity to unite against common enemies and the possibilities of negotiating to avoid conflict, the realization that true friends outweigh any material hoarding. More than ever, as the world approaches a tipping point where the destruction caused by non-adaptive behaviour is liable to sweep all before it, we need these qualities. Seeing them played out on the savannah in that magical early light, with Amiguete tending his foals as a flock of scarlet ibis leaves its roost, Gitana raising her head as a giant anteater wafts its feathery way past the grazing herd, the Latin Kings kneeling with their rumps in the air in yet another game, and the slow, synchronized drift of the bands merging and swaying apart again, is to be overwhelmed by the sense of harmony and peace that is the essence of horse. We have a lot to learn, not just about them but *from* them. Inside every domestic horse is a feral one with the same certainty about how life should be lived.

# Notes and References

## Chapter 1

[1]  A popular form of "round pen" training starts with chasing the horse (negative punishment) until he gives signals of relaxation and allows the trainer to approach. The horse may be further punished for not following the trainer. This is not voluntary action. Chasing is unnecessary and, in the case of a frightened horse, exacerbates his fear. If we wish the horse to come to us, chasing him away is illogical.

[2]  Tinbergen 1963.

[3]  Sociobiology is the study of the ways in which a species' evolutionary adaptation to a particular ecological niche influences social organization: see Wilson, 1975.

[4]  Maynard Smith and Price 1973; Maynard Smith 1982, a book in which he introduced the idea of an evolutionarily stable strategy (ESS). An ESS is a set of behaviours conserved over evolutionary time because it cannot be bettered, like horses' flight from strange moving objects that might turn out to be predators.

[5]  Lee Dugatkin has shown how an animal's decision as to whether or not to fight is affected by its previous experience.  Dugatkin and Druen 2004, Dugatkin and Earley 2004.

[6]  See, for instance, www.ethologicalethics.org, the web page of the organization Ethologists for the Ethical Treatment of Animals. Bekoff has published several books on this subject: a good one is Bekoff 2003.

[7]  Harlow showed that contact, rather then food-providing, played the major role in care-giving, the development of love and normal social behaviour: see, for instance H. Harlow 1958. The descriptions of the baby monkeys' distress are upsetting, especially because Harlow deliberately used everyday emotive words like love instead of the scientific term 'affective bond', which distances us from the animal's experience.

[8]  Le Doux's book (1998) is an excellent exposition of complicated neurology written in clear, easily understood terms by the leading researcher in this field.

[9]  Which makes the deliberate infliction of pain and suffering on animals to satisfy our own ambitions, for instance in equestrian 'sport' and pleasure riding, clearly cruel. Harlow's work has also been heavily criticised for the suffering he inflicted. Yet it clarified how to prevent and alleviate further suffering, for instance in the thousands of babies found in Romanian orphanages without any care except feeding and cleaning, after the collapse of Ceaucescu's regime. Now that his discoveries have passed into the sphere of generally accepted knowledge, it is difficult to remember that, at the time, they were indeed discoveries. Whether that justifies his experiments or not is a matter of ethics, a question on which scientific attitudes have changed enormously, partly as a result of them.

[10]  A classic on the subject is Panksepp 1998.

## Chapter 2

[11]  Robin Dunbar first proposed his 'social brain hypothesis' in 1998, comparing data on neocortex size in primate groups.

[12]  Schultz and Dunbar 2006 extends the social brain hypothesis to ungulates.

[13]  For the best modern review of horse evolution see Bruce McFadden 1993, which clearly shows that horse evolution does not take the straight line that creationists love to attack, but resembles more a branching tree whose ramifications die out or continue according to the lines' adaptability to climatic and ecological changes.

## Chapter 3

[14]  The references for this chapter are numerous and I have jumped from one to another often in producing this summary. Here they are listed briefly according to where the study took place, with mention of special interest studies, while complete references are given in the reference list.

*General overviews:* Linklater 2000; Rubenstein 1986, 1994.

*England:* Tyler 1972.

*Camargue, France:* Boy and Duncan 1979, 1980 (time-budgets); Duncan *et al.* 1984 (inbreeding reduction); Monard *et al.* 1996 (natal dispersal); Wells & von Goldsmidt-Rothschild 1979.

*Spain:* Rifa 1990 (synchrony); Lagos 2013 (wolf predation)

*Canada, western:* Salter 1979, Salter & Hudson 1982.

*Canada, Sable Island:* Welsh 1973.

*USA mustangs:* Berger 1977, 1986; Boyd 1980; Feist & McCullough 1976; Miller & Denniston 1979 (interband competition); Miller 1981; Pelligrini 1971.

*USA east-coast island ponies:* Keiper 1985; Rubenstein 1981; Rubenstein & Hack 1992 (stallion conflict); Rutberg 1990 (transfer); Rutberg & Greenberg 1990 (aggression); Rutberg & Keiper 1993 (natal dispersal); Stevens 1990.

*Iceland:* Granquist et al. 2012

*Japanese island horses:* Kaseda 1983; Kaseda et al. 1995; Kaseda & Nosawa 1996;

Kaseda *et al.* 1997 (a series of papers on influences on breeding success).

*New Zealand:* Linklater et al. 1999; Linklater & Cameron 2000; Linklater et al. 2000.

[15] The immunocontraception of feral mares with porcine zona pellucida extract (PZP) is now common in the USA. Nuñez *et al.* (2014), working on Shackleford Banks, went on to show that treated mares showed high levels of stress due to their frequent band changes. Any mare, on changing bands, is subject to both stallion harassment and aggression from the resident mares for a couple of weeks.

[16] In domestic horses inbreeding is common, either in managed matings or because the horses have no alternative partners. However, I have known colts who grew to maturity alone with their mothers to be so frightened of in-season mares that they could not mate: their mothers had refused them so often and fiercely that the smell of an in-season mare put them off entirely.

[17] The Kaimanawa horses numbered 1,576 in 1994. Their range is used for Army manoeuvres, and the population was also mustered. During musters, bands are broken up and lose members indiscriminately. Such disruptions affect social relations, especially aggressiveness in stallions.

[18] In Spain, acorns are normally not poisonous. Whether this is because of our species of oak (*Quercus pirenaica, Q. ilex*) or because the acorns are mature and brown before they fall I am not sure, but think the latter. Acorns and chestnuts do have a worming effect.

[19] Names. Ethologists need to identify individual animals, and at first did so with impersonal letters and numbers like M32 or Bb4. Jane Goodall broke with tradition and gave her chimps names, a precedent most of us now follow. On finding a new feral population I usually call the first male I see a name beginning with A, the second with B and so on. The mares with him have names beginning with the same letter, which gets complicated if they change bands. The Camoruco stallions are so numerous and have such a fast turnover that when one dies his letter is re-used for a new one. My pottoka nomenclature looks hopelessly haphazard since the founder members came with registered names and their offspring are given Basque names.

## Chapter 4

[20] In this account I have not considered the possibility of horses attacking predators because I have never seen it happen. Horses do not attack puma, though some astonishing photos on the Internet showed a mule attacking and killing one. But there are numerous anecdotal accounts of pony stallions in northern Spain rushing to attack wolves, and the pottokas, both stallions and mares, chase off dogs. In Wales, pony stallions sometimes kill lambs by stomping on them. There is a possibility that this defensive attack of smaller animals is the origin of foal-killing in stallions stressed by confinement (Ch. 3) and the occasional report of stallions attacking fallen people.

Both donkeys and mules show this behaviour more than do horses, and in Leon, donkey stallions are increasingly used to protect herds against wolves.

[21] These observations agree with those of other researchers: Boy and Duncan, Rifa, Feist and McCullough.

[22] A horse immersed in pain often holds his head in the vigilant position, though he shows no other signs of vigilance: his ears hang sideways, the eyes are unfocused and the mouth slack, although the nostrils are flared. These contradictory signs should alert our suspicions.

[23] In the ridden horse this position is called 'inverted'. Increasing pressure on the mouth, or pulling the reins alternately, do nothing to diminish the fear or discomfort that produce the position.

[24] Tame horses, when led, tend to crowd us when startled, too.

[25] Miriam Homedes Palau (2014) made simultaneous recordings of heart rate variation and expressions in horses in fearful situations. They show that these are accurate readings of fear.

## Chapter 5

[26] This side-to-side movement is reproduced at high speed during weaving in stressed stabled horses who cannot graze.

## Chapter 6

[27] They seem to be wising up. While in 2013 and 2014 they grazed mostly in the valleys and lost almost all their foals, in 2016 they were found more on the heights, and there were three yearlings as well as a two-year-old and 10 foals,

though how many of these survived I do not know. The puma had multiplied.

The behavioural adaptations necessary for successful feralization are not well studied but cannot include recovery of genes lost during domestication: rather, they seem to depend on experience during key developmental stages and its subsequent cultural transmission to offspring.

[28] In Patagonia I found the skeletons of two young males, aged six and seven, with broken incisors, and one of my founder pottoka stallions, Hodei, died as a result of a broken, infected incisor. Previous to his decline we had seen him chasing the bachelor Pintxo, who was persistently harassing the band and who defended himself during the chases with kicks at Hodei´s face.

Interestingly, Hodei made no attempt to defend his daughters against Pintxo´s intrusions, only the mares. Pintxo did not seem to realize why Hodei sometimes tolerated him and sometimes attacked him.

[29] The news is bad. Because of Chavez's death and the subsequent social unrest I have not returned to the Hato and have been unable to complete the studies I planned. The administrator told us that in 2013 only forty-eight horses, including foals, remained. A severe El Niño in 2014 did not help. While we all cherish hopes for their survival, I fear for them. Dr. Vargas said in 2016 that they were "recovering" but gave no details of numbers.

All who went on these courses remain deeply impressed by our privilege and the understanding that this herd and the glory of their surroundings gave us.

[30] While testosterone provides libido to perform, many patterns of behaviour characteristic of stallions are perfected by learning and practice. Some geldings, cut late after practising stallion behaviours like herding, court-ing or mounting mares, continue to do them after being gelded, though not with the same fervour as before. This often puzzles their owners. I had a Welsh pony who, gelded at six years old after running with mares, still mounted them at the age of over thirty.

[31] Lagos, L. 2013. The ponies Lagos studied now lose about half their foals to wolves, partly because other usual sources of food like dead stock are no longer available. Lagos found that mares who lived in close association with others were less likely to lose their foals, but there was only slight advantage in close association with a stallion. Since there were only three stallions, one of whom did not flourish, and up to twenty-seven mares with each, no conclusions can be drawn from her figures: a similar study on truly feral, unmanaged horses would be welcome.

[32] Curiously, once when I rode past his band on a gelding, Hodei rushed out and tried to herd a pile of dung away from us, repeatedly and furiously; when we moved away he was perfectly friendly to the gelding, whom he had not met before.

Free-living stallions often terrify passing riders by rushing to examine their horses, but unless you are on a stallion or an in-season mare problems are unlikely: once the stallion has smelled a gelding he realizes there is no testoster-one and is more likely to treat him as a foal.

## Chapter 7

[33] For some of the many discussions on what dominance actually means, either theoretically or in terms of the daily lives of animals, see:

de Waal 2007; Dunbar 1988; Estevez et al. 2007; Fraser 1985; Hediger 1955; Hinde 1978; Jensen 1982; Kolter 1984; Wilson 1974.

[34] For instance, when dominance assessment includes herding, stallions rank higher than when it does not.

[35] For instance Goodwin 2002.

A submissive gesture inhibits the aggression of another: "don't attack, I give up now." Horses have no way of switching off another's aggression. This is just as well, for in the confusion of terror they might try to signal submis-sion to an attacking predator. Escape is always a better strategy.

Many think that the "snapping" mouth movements given by foals to adults, especially to stallions, signal submis-sion. Crowell-Davis and others showed that, although adults are seldom aggressive to foals that approach them, a foal's snapping does not prevent aggression if the adult is annoyed. I once saw a foal snapping so persistently at a stallion that the latter finally drove him away aggressively; I have also seen a pottoka foal snap at an electric fence. What exactly the gesture means is not clear, but the posture adopted, with bent knees and outstretched neck, resembles that of a suckling foal. Given that foals when frightened rush to their mothers for a few seconds' non-nutritive suckling, snapping may be a redirected form of this response to fear. The fact that foals stop snapping at around a year old unless really terrified supports this idea.

Monty Roberts proposed that "licking and chewing" mouth movements and lowering the head to the ground are submission signals. Both are seen when the horse has been tense for some minutes, with the jaw, neck and back muscles in constant, uncomfortable contraction and his mouth dried by adrenaline. As his tension passes he works these muscles to recover the blood flow in them, just as we wriggle our shoulders after putting down a heavy load that has required sustained effort to maintain; licking helps restore saliva flow too.

Roberts probably based his idea on the observation that a tense horse is unresponsive. Tense muscles contract further when pressure is applied due to the activation of the stretch reflex. This reflex is necessary for instance in walking, when our leg muscles push back against the ground matching the load put on them. Activation of the stretch reflex makes a tense horse push back against the pressures that are our aids, appearing resistant. A horse that has relaxed is more likely to push to pressure, as we want. This is another example of correct observation but faulty interpretation. "The horse is an into-pressure animal" is only true if the horse is tense.

Horses that have begun work in a relaxed frame of mind do not give these signals unless they subsequently become tense and then relax again. Dressage horses working hard are encouraged to walk with the head stretched down for a minute from time to time, to stretch and relieve the back muscles. Riding school horses made rigid by pushing against constant, heavy rein pressure often try to stretch their backs by throwing their heads down in the same way, but are thought to be being rebellious, not submissive.

[36] Displays of this type call attention to an animal's strength and agility, and are used in various contexts: in conflict, to avoid fighting ('Don't fight with me: you'll lose'); in courtship ('Mate with me to have great offspring'), and, in some species like Thomson's gazelle, to predators ('Don't bother chasing me, I'll escape easily'). We should not equate such displays with conflict.

[37] Sheep and goats, too, distinguish between momentary social annoyances ('go-away' signals) and conflicts that establish dominance-submission relations. They do have a specific submission signal but only use it in male-male fights (Shackleton and Shanks 1984).

[38] For a good review of recent work that takes this view of aggression, see Fureix *et al.* 2012.

[39] Quoted in Fureix *et al.* Stebbins' Ph.D. thesis is widely quoted but difficult to get.

[40] Aggression frequencies on Assateague are anyway higher than in most feral populations, perhaps owing to overcrowding and perhaps to competition for handouts and garbage.

## Chapter 8

[41] Nuclear physicists manage to use *charm* and *spin* without creating so much confusion, but a) they define what they mean by them and b) their subject is less popular.

[42] Drews' definition is structural: it defines an observed consistency in conflictive encounters. It does not imply that this has any social function. Nevertheless, in many papers, researchers use the definition, create a data hierarchy, and promptly set about trying to find a function for it.

[43] I do not mean to single out these writers for special criticism: the misunderstanding is common. However they are all well-known writers who have tried to establish that their views are scientifically valid.

[44] Horse-keepers do find a considerable reduction in aggression when "slow feeders" are used in groups, but the only research I can find is on the use of slow feeders in stables (Hallam *et al.* 2012). They found a reduction in stereotypic behaviour and a normalization of time budgets.

[45] The *llaneros* in Venezuela made the same mistake. 'The stallions are always fighting', they told us when we first arrived. We never saw stallions fight, but the bachelors play ceaselessly.

[46] Milgram, like many others, was interested in why so many people participated in the institutionalised cruelty of the Holocaust. His experiment was apparently directed at learning lists of words. The volunteers were apparently randomly divided into subjects and experimenters, the subject being strapped into a chair through which an electric current could be delivered by the experimenter when the subject gave the wrong answer. A dial showed the current delivered; the lowest values corresponded to mere tingling, higher values to painful shock and the highest to extreme pain causing convulsions and temporary black-out. Experimenters were told to increase the current for every successive mistake. Two-thirds did so up to the highest values without objecting; some protested but nevertheless carried on, but very few refused to deliver what appeared to be painful shocks.

In fact the ballot system for assigning subject or experimenter role was rigged. All the 'subjects' were actors and there was no current, though the experimenters did not know this. The actors screamed, pleaded and convulsed as the current apparently increased.

Milgram's results horrified psychologists unwilling to accept that ordinary Americans were capable of such behaviour. He was attacked for misleading the volunteers and for possibly choosing an atypical simple of volunteers (college students, thought in the 1950s to be more obedient than the general populace). However, the experiment has since been repeated several times with the same results.

## Chapter 9

[47] For instance the percentage of healthy sperm in a previously sub-fertile Colombian paso fino stallion, difficult and dangerous to handle, improved by 40 per cent by changing his night-time stable and turning him out daily in a paddock next to playful sons; he could be handled without difficulty, ridden out with others, and the children played with him in the paddock. Vets frequently comment on the rapid improvements they see when we find the right place and conditions for stallions, but seldom give me hard figures.

# Index